VOL. 162

HAL•LEONARD®

GUITAR PLAY-ALONG

AUDIO ACCESS INCLUDED

EAGLES HITS

CONTENTS

To access audio, visit:
www.halleonard.com/mylibrary

Enter Code
4381-3948-6474-8758

Cover photo: © MartyTemme
MartyTemmeArchives.com

ISBN 978-1-4768-1413-1

HAL•LEONARD®

Visit Hal Leonard Online at
www.halleonard.com

World headquarters, contact:
Hal Leonard
7777 West Bluemound Road
Milwaukee, WI 53213
Email: info@halleonard.com

In Europe, contact:
Hal Leonard Europe Limited
1 Red Place
London, W1K 6PL
Email: info@halleonardeurope.com

In Australia, contact:
Hal Leonard Australia Pty. Ltd.
4 Lentara Court
Cheltenham, Victoria, 3192 Australia
Email: info@halleonard.com.au

Already Gone

Words and Music by Jack Tempchin and Robb Strandlund

Intro
Moderately fast Rock ♩ = 144

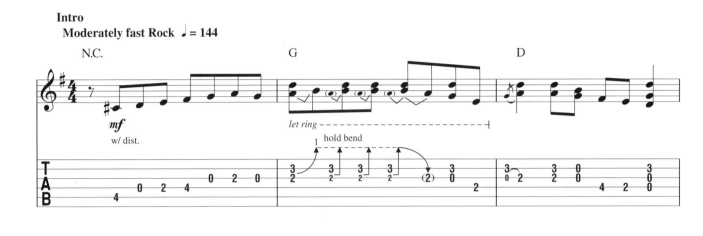

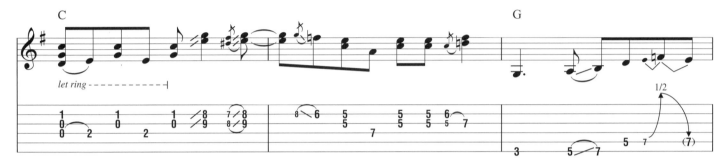

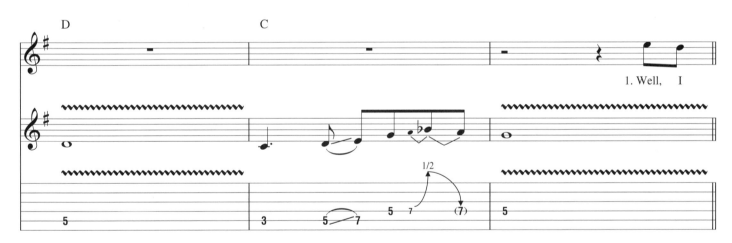

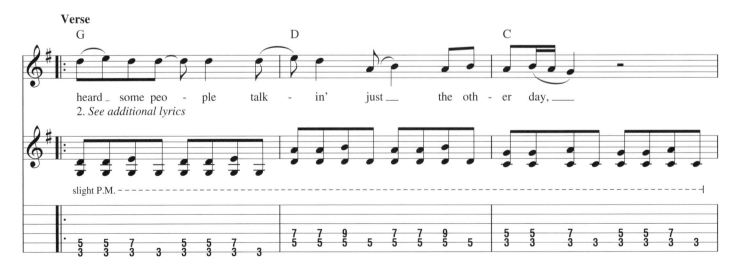

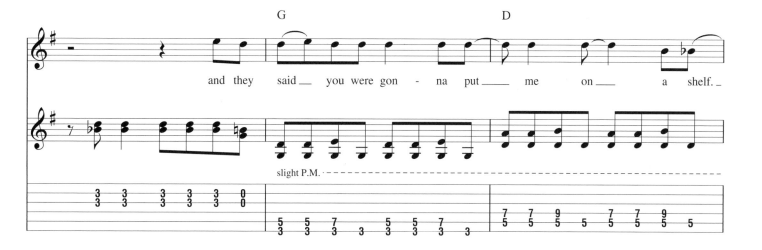

and they said __ you were gon - na put __ me on __ a shelf. __

2nd time, substitute Fill 1

But let me tell you, I got some news __ for you, __

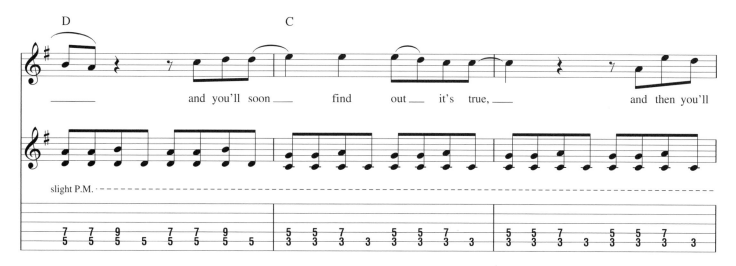

and you'll soon __ find out __ it's true, __ and then you'll

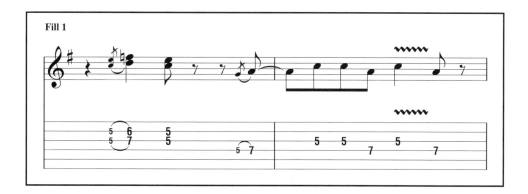

Fill 1

2nd time, substitute Fill 2

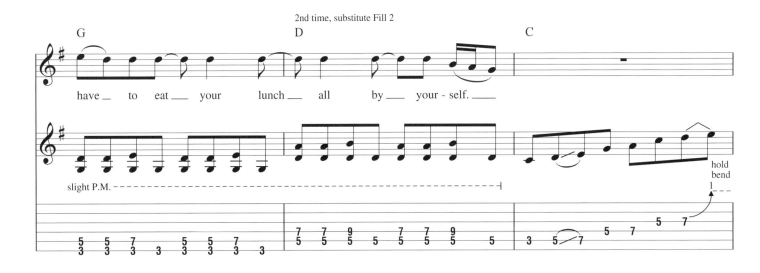

have __ to eat __ your __ lunch __ all __ by __ your - self. __

Chorus

'Cause And } I'm al - read - y gone, __

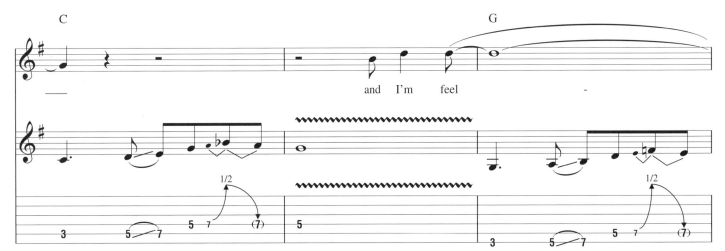

— and I'm feel -

Fill 2

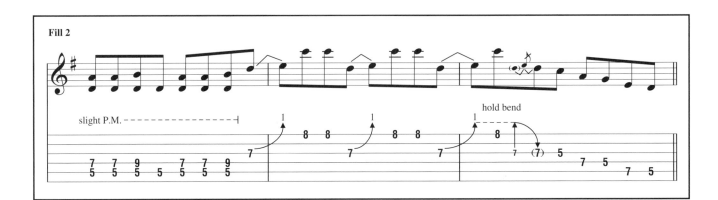

4

2nd time, substitute Fill 3

in' strong. ___

2nd time, substitute Fill 4

this vic - t'ry song. ___

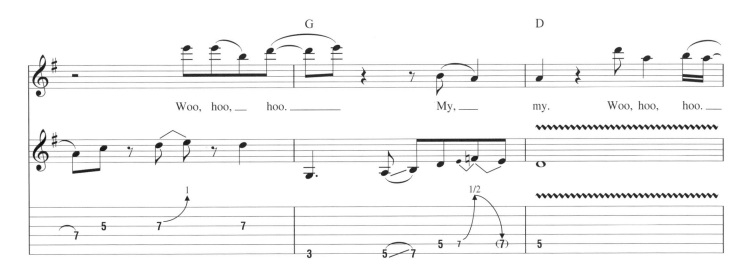

Woo, hoo, ___ hoo. ___   My, ___ my.   Woo, hoo, hoo. ___

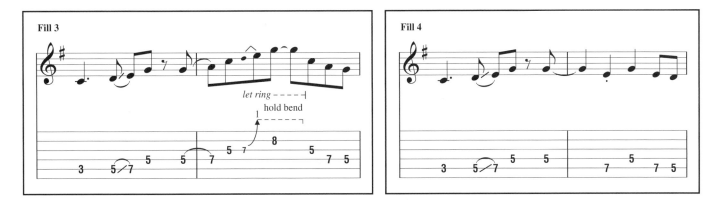

Fill 3

let ring
hold bend

Fill 4

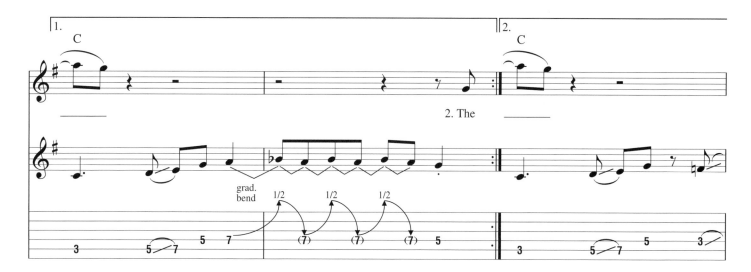

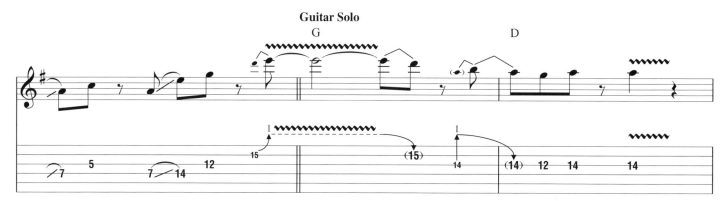

Guitar Solo

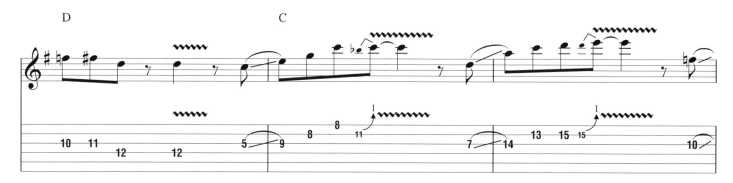

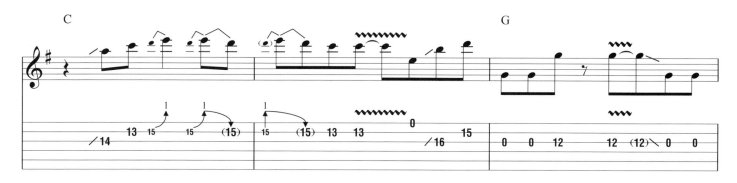

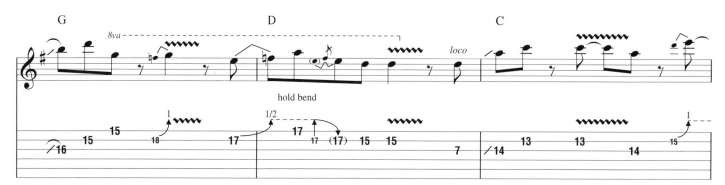

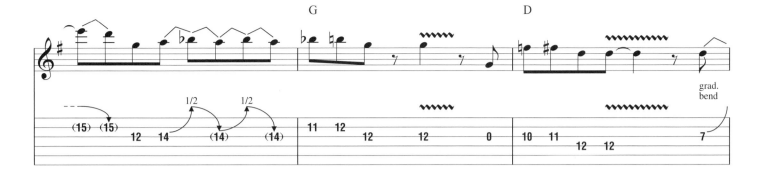

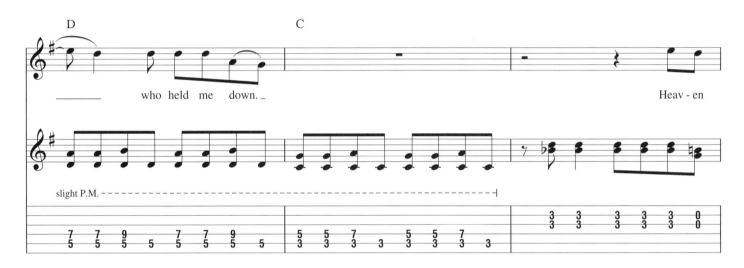

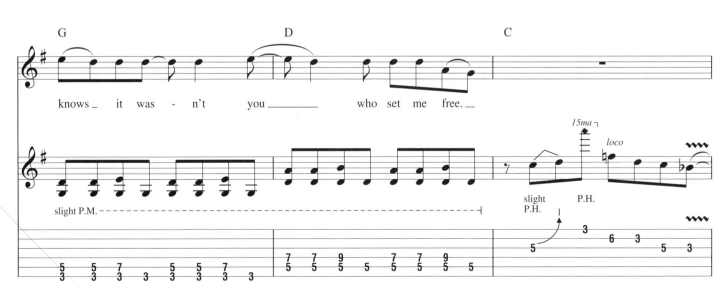

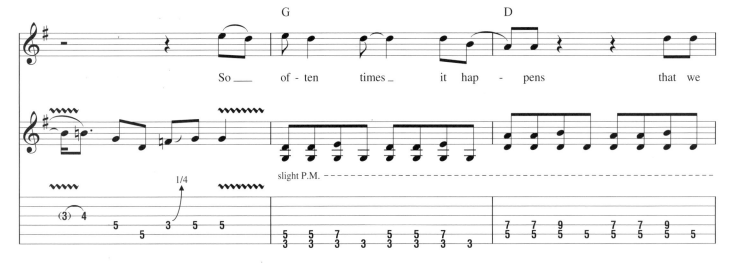

So __ of - ten times __ it hap - pens that we

live our lives in chains, __ and we nev - er e - ven know __

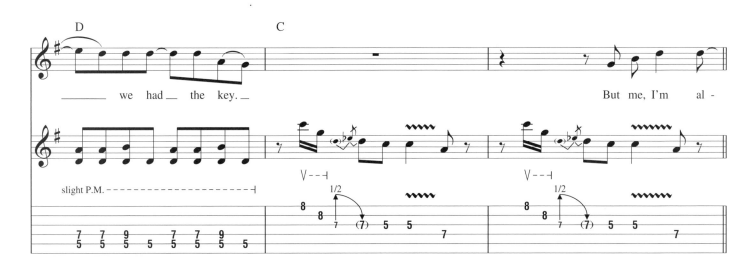

_____ we had __ the key. __ But me, I'm al -

Chorus

- read - y gone, __ and I'm feel-

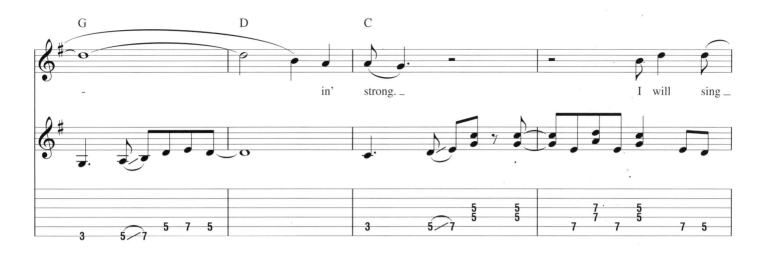

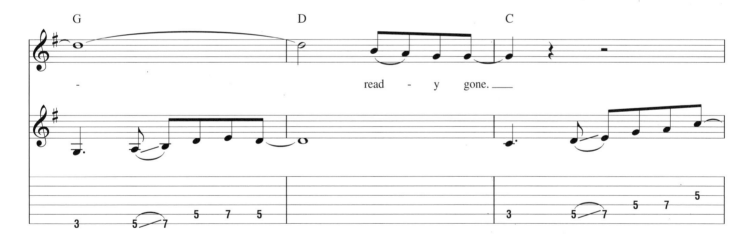

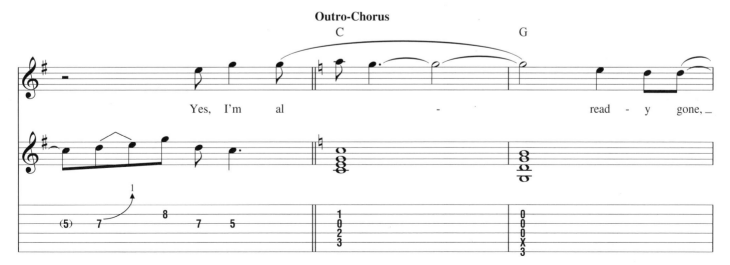

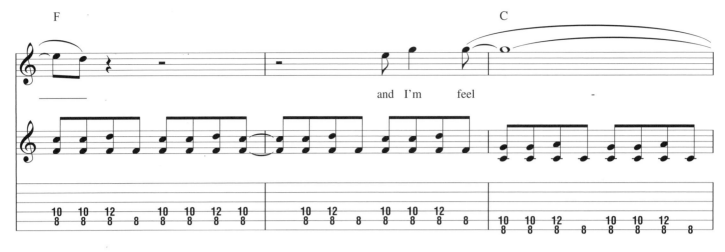

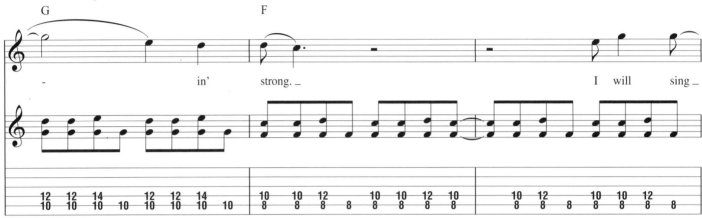

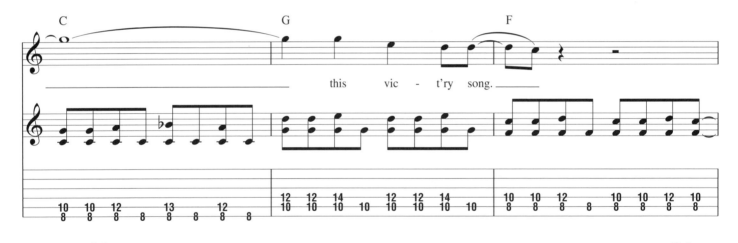

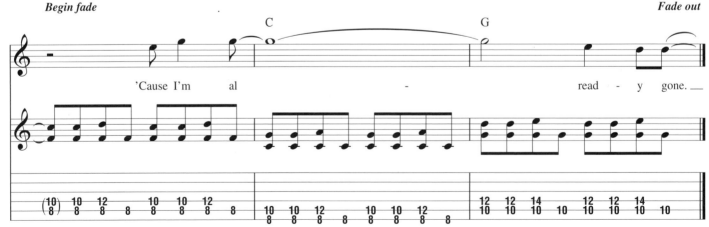

Additional Lyrics

2. The letter that you wrote me made me stop and wonder why,
But I guess you felt like you had to set things right.
Just remember this, my girl, when you look up in the sky:
You could see the stars and still not see the light. That's right.

Heartache Tonight

Words and Music by John David Souther, Don Henley, Glenn Frey and Bob Seger

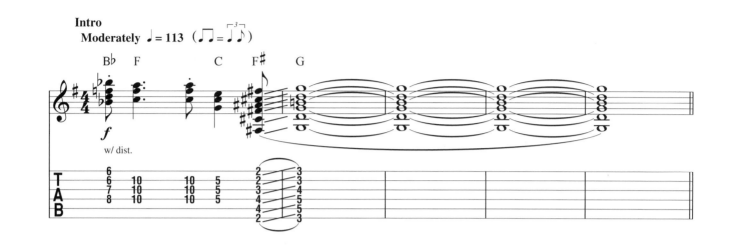

11

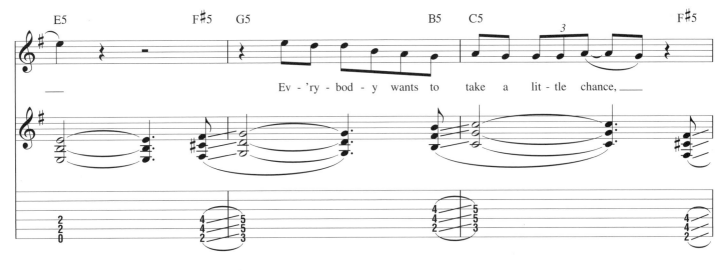

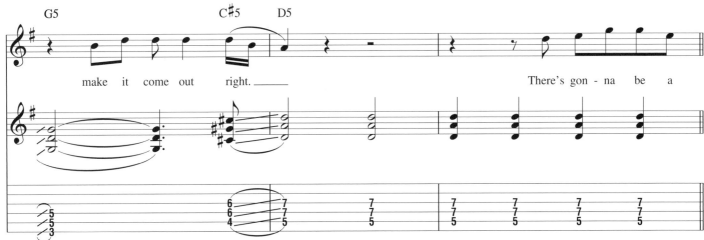

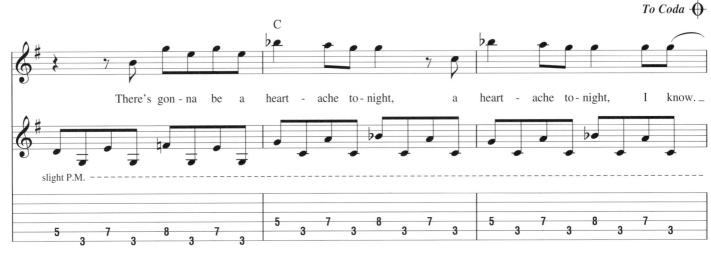

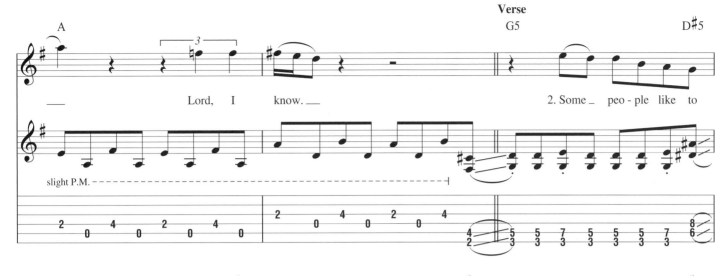

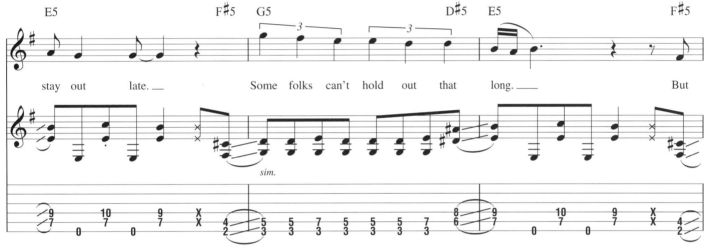

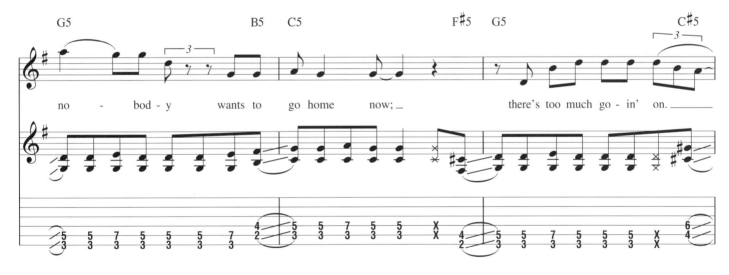

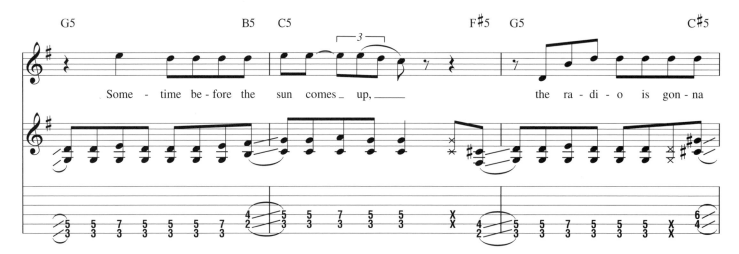

Chorus

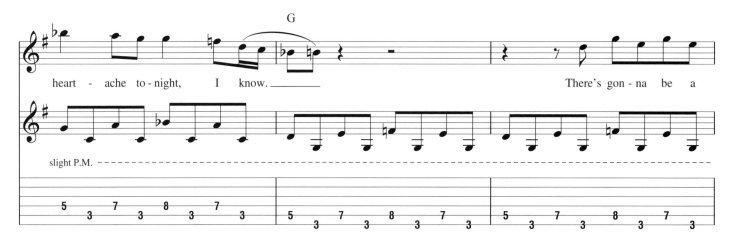

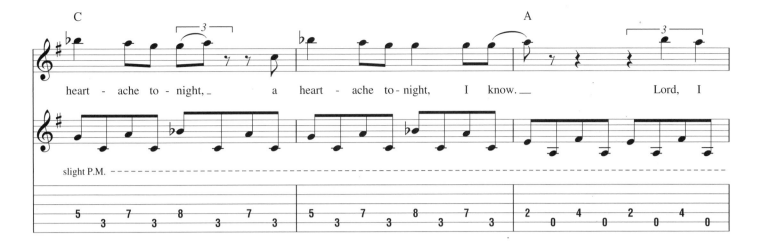

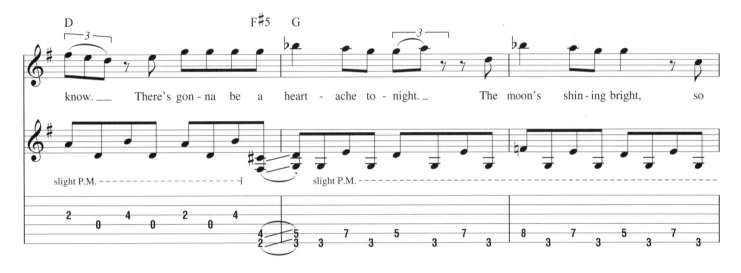

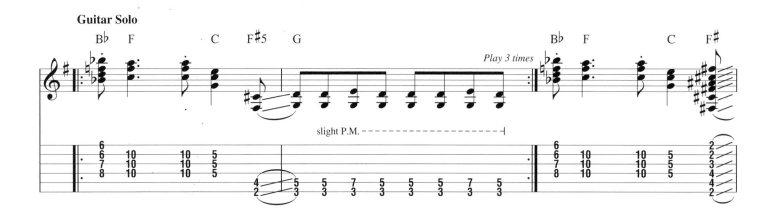

Guitar Solo

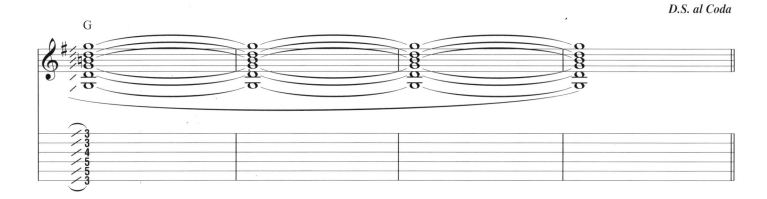

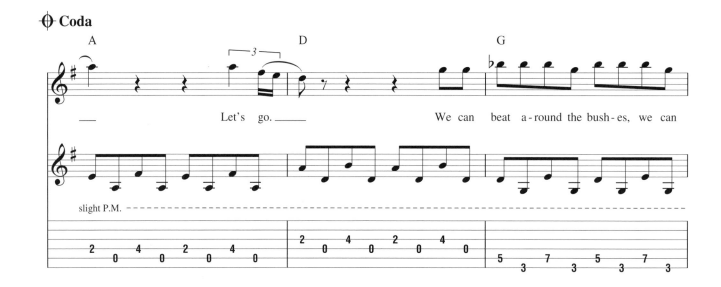

𝄌 Coda

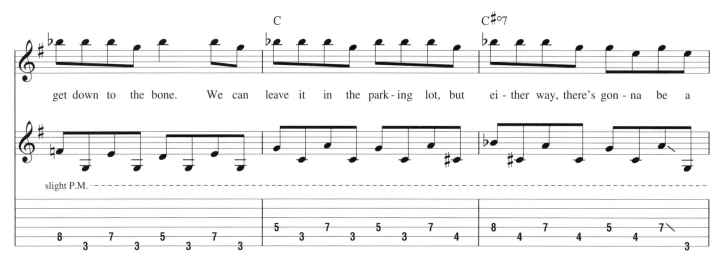

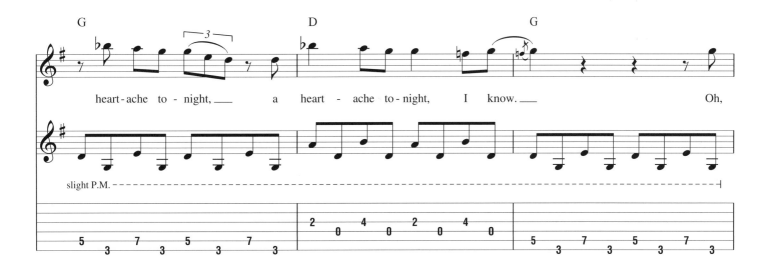

heart-ache to-night, ___ a heart-ache to-night, I know. ___ Oh,

I know. ___ There'll be a heart - ache to-night, ___ a heart-ache to-night, I know. ___

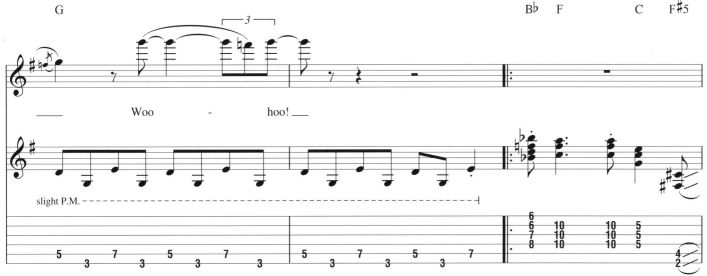

Woo - hoo! ___

Outro

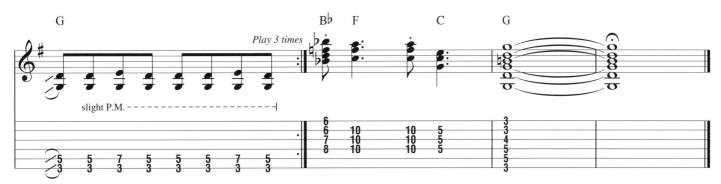

Play 3 times

Hotel California

Words and Music by Don Henley, Glenn Frey and Don Felder

Intro

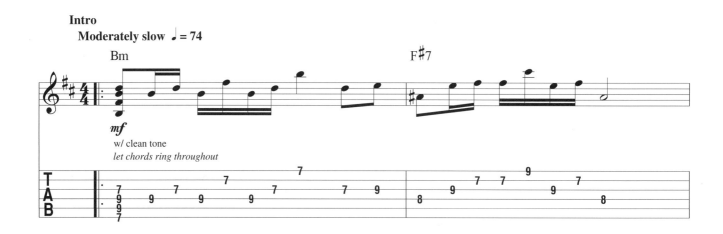

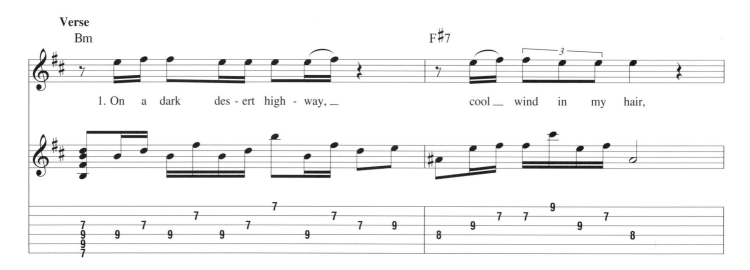

Verse

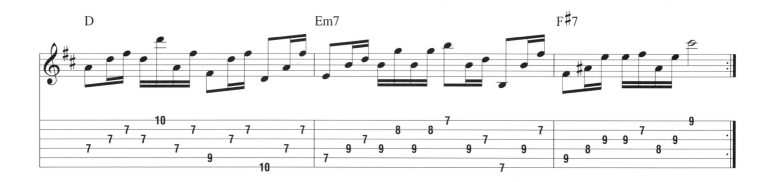

1. On a dark des-ert high-way, ___ cool ___ wind in my hair,

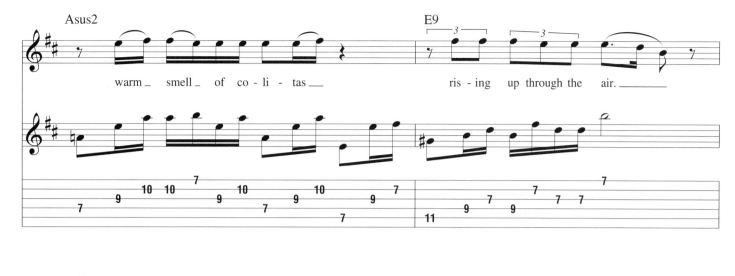

warm _ smell _ of co - li - tas _ ris - ing up through the air. _____

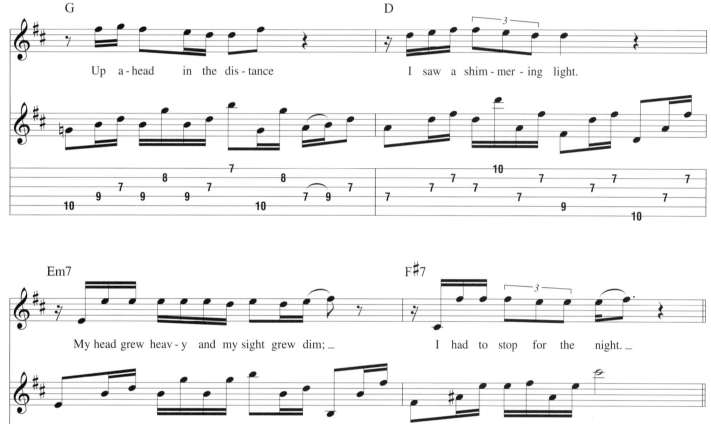

Up a - head in the dis - tance I saw a shim - mer - ing light.

My head grew heav - y and my sight grew dim; _ I had to stop for the night. _

Verse

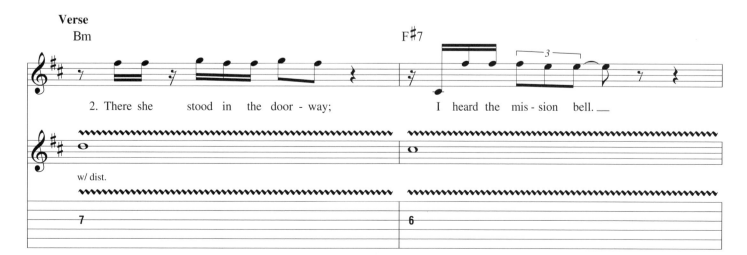

2. There she stood in the door - way; I heard the mis - sion bell. _

w/ dist.

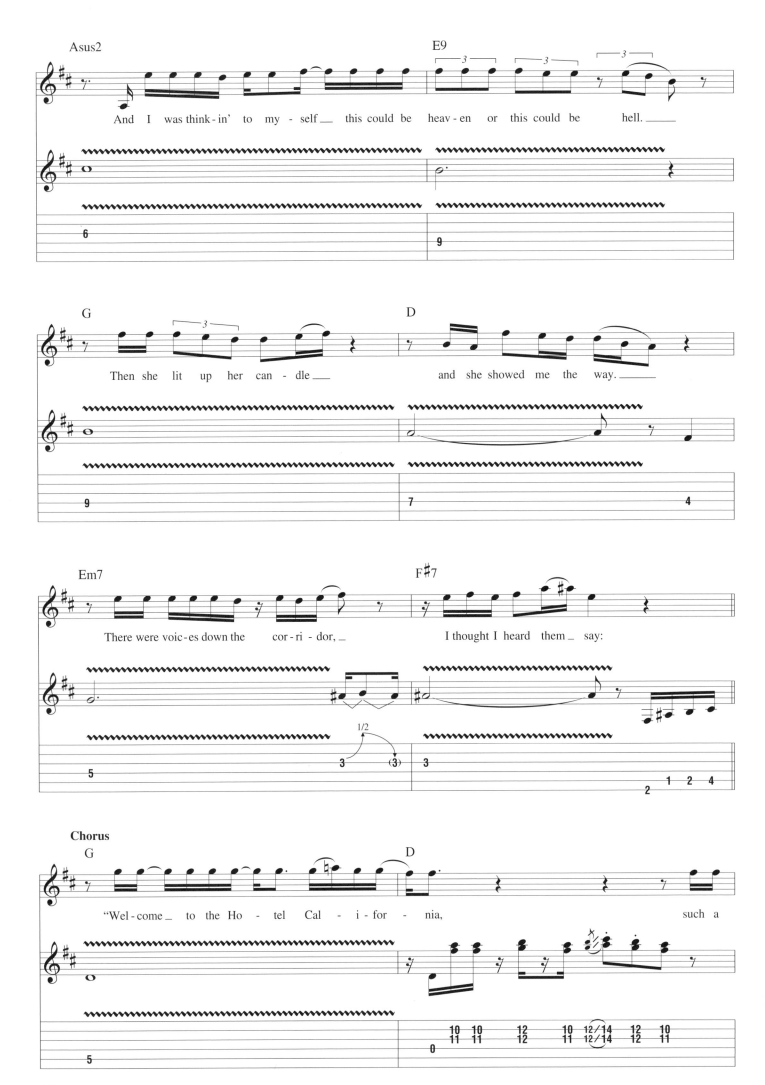

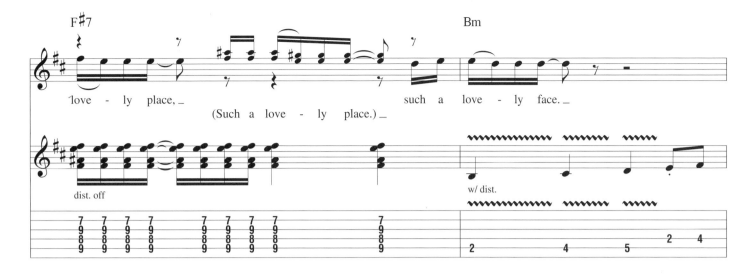

love - ly place, ___ (Such a love - ly place.) ___ such a love - ly face. ___

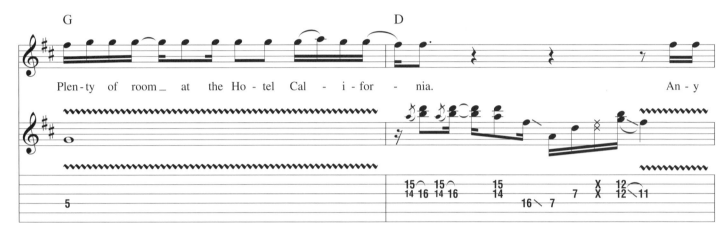

Plen - ty of room ___ at the Ho - tel Cal - i - for - nia. An - y

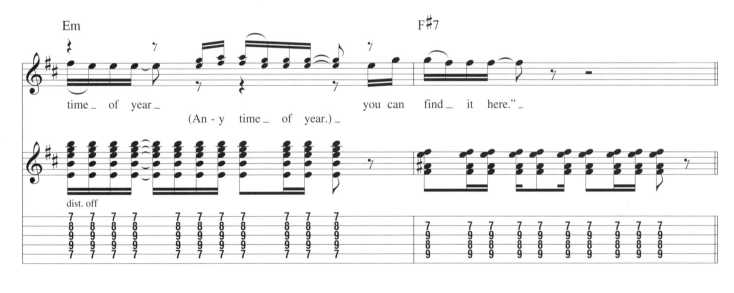

time ___ of year ___ (An - y time ___ of year.) ___ you can find ___ it here." ___

Verse

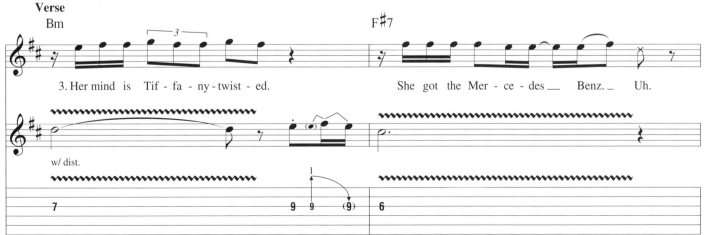

3. Her mind is Tif - fa - ny - twist - ed. She got the Mer - ce - des ___ Benz. ___ Uh.

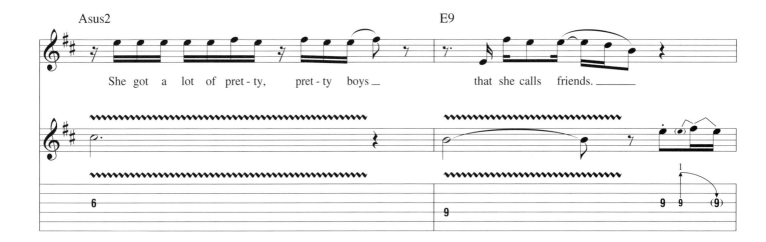

She got a lot of pret-ty, pret-ty boys _____ that she calls friends. _____

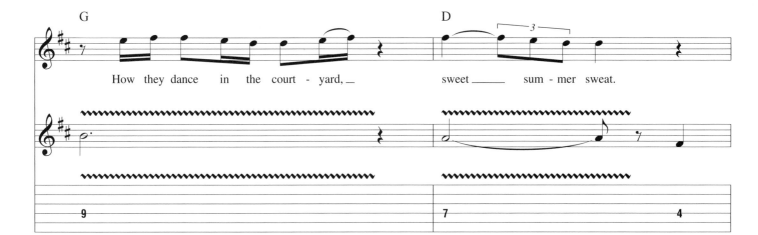

How they dance in the court - yard, _ sweet _____ sum - mer sweat.

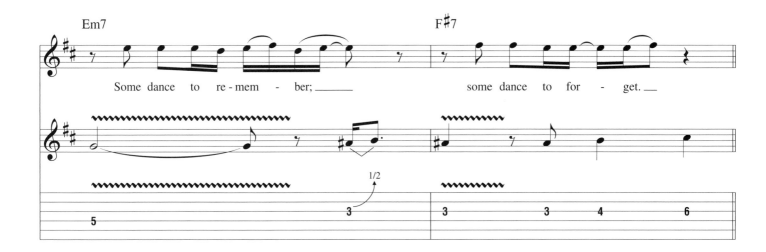

Some dance to re - mem - ber; _____ some dance to for - get. _

Verse

4. So I _____ called up the cap - tain, "Please bring me my _____ wine." _ He said,

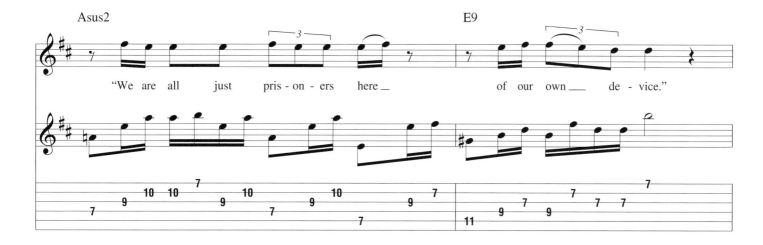

Asus2   E9

"We are all just pris - on - ers here ___ of our own ___ de - vice."

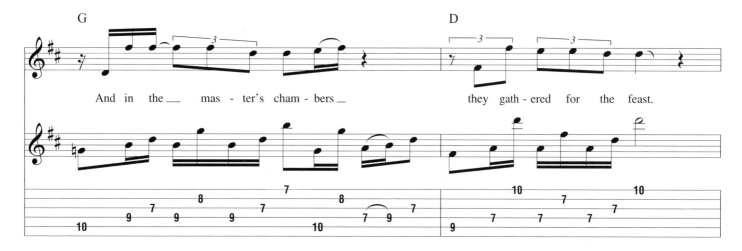

G   D

And in the ___ mas - ter's cham - bers ___ they gath - ered for the feast.

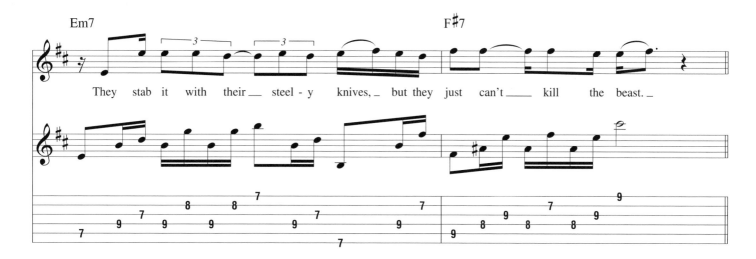

Em7   F#7

They stab it with their ___ steel - y knives, _ but they just can't ___ kill the beast. _

Verse

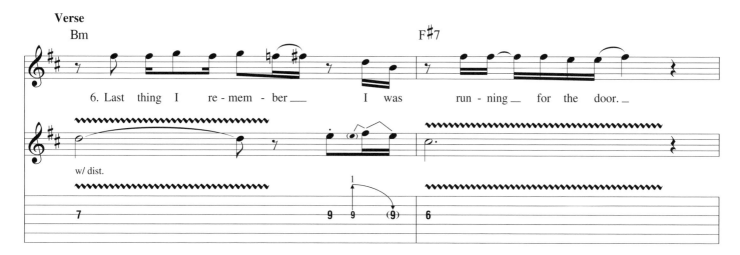

Bm   F#7

6. Last thing I re - mem - ber ___ I was run - ning ___ for the door. _

w/ dist.

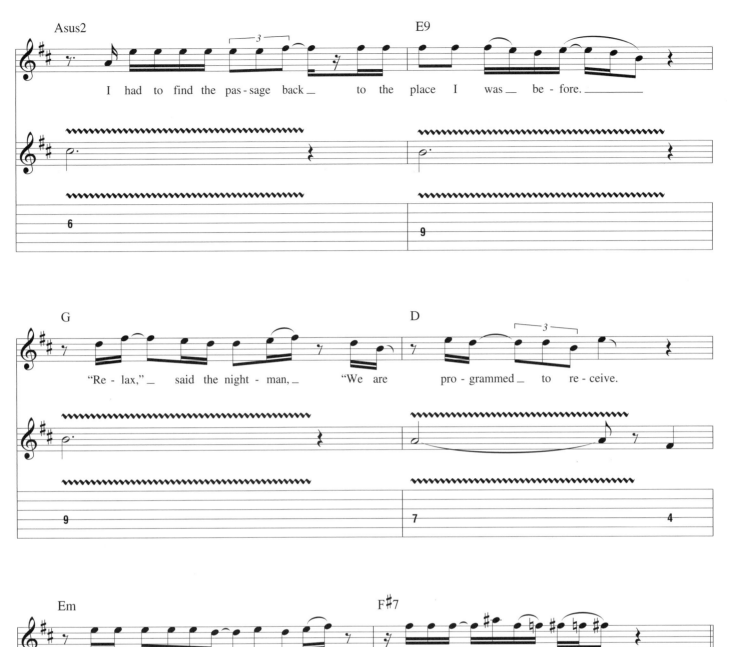

Asus2   E9

I had to find the pas-sage back __ to the place I was __ be-fore. _____

G   D

"Re - lax," __ said the night-man, __ "We are pro-grammed __ to re-ceive.

Em   F#7

You can check out an - y __ time you like __ but you can __ nev - er __ leave." __

Guitar Solo

Bm   F#7

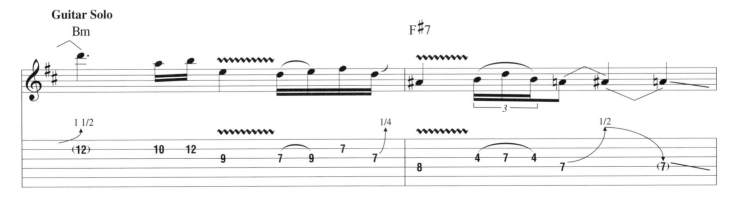

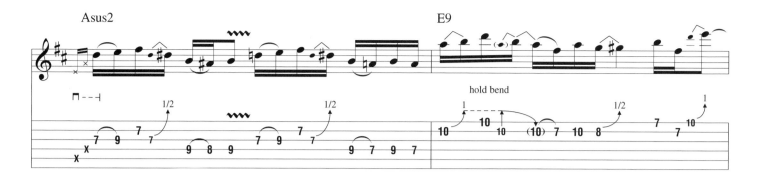

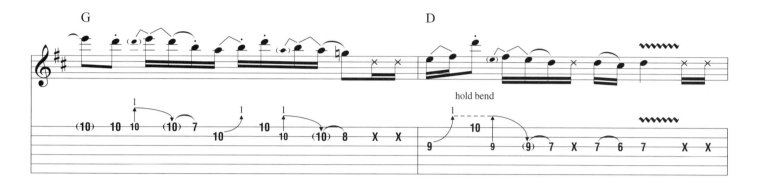

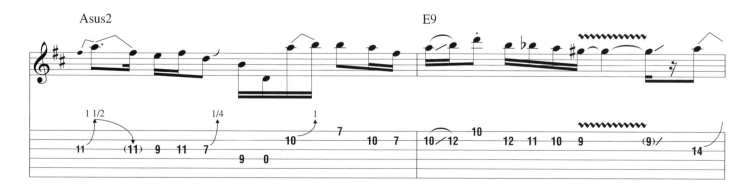

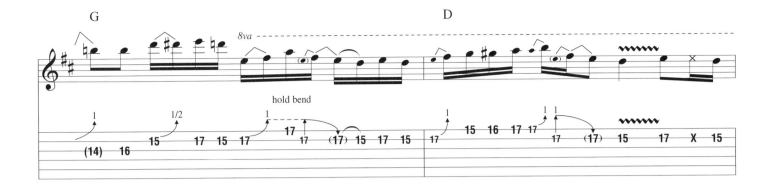

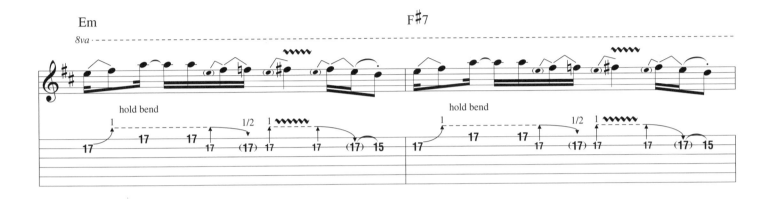

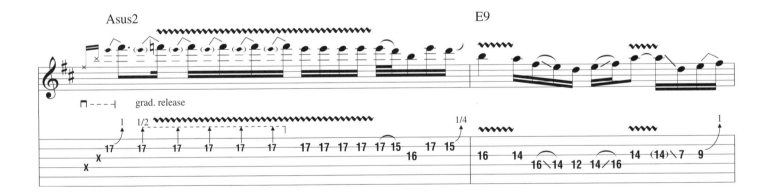

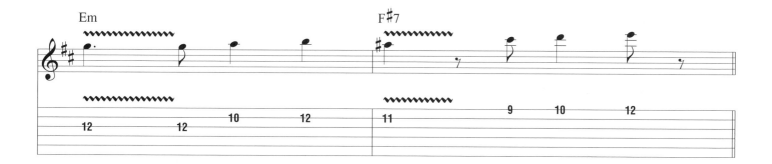

Outro

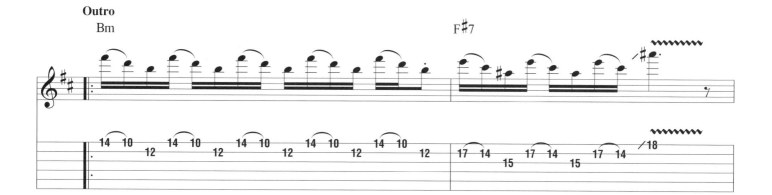

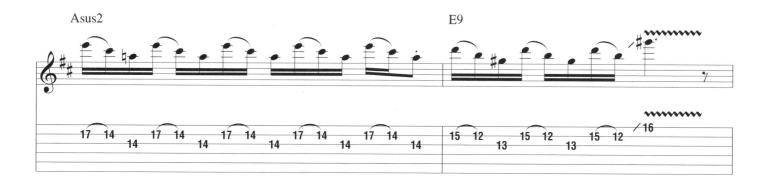

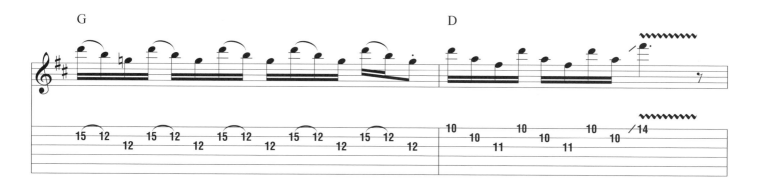

Repeat and fade

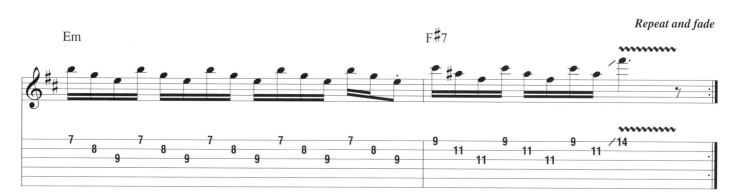

Life in the Fast Lane

Words and Music by Don Henley, Glenn Frey and Joe Walsh

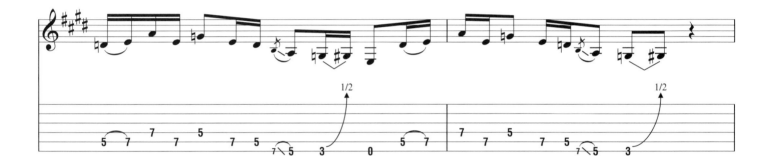

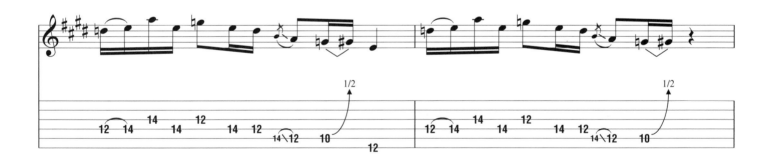

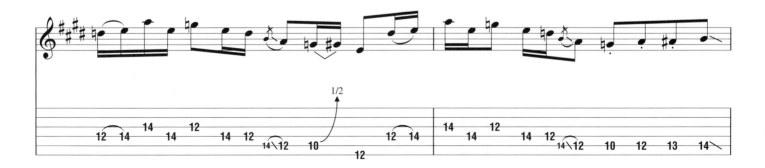

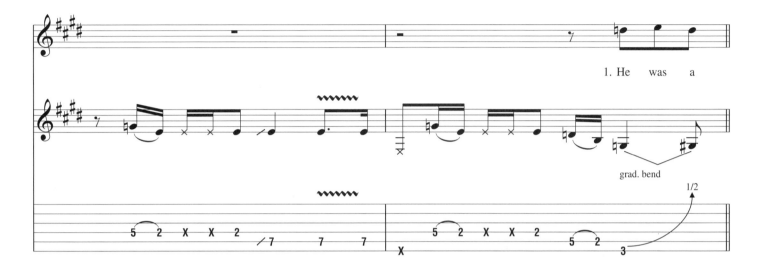

1. He was a

Verse

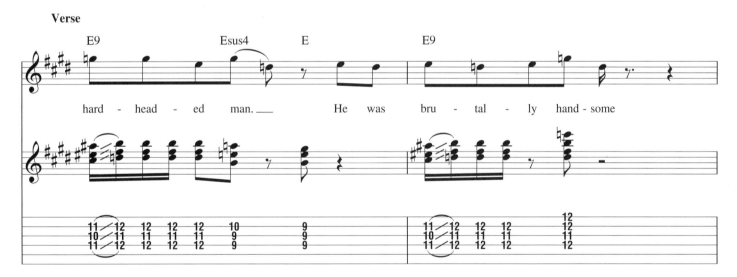

hard - head - ed man. ___ He was bru - tal - ly hand - some

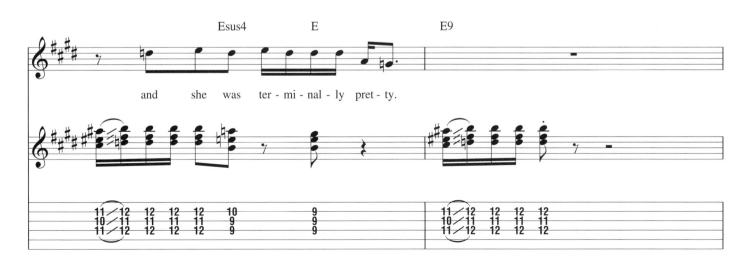

and she was ter - mi - nal - ly pret - ty.

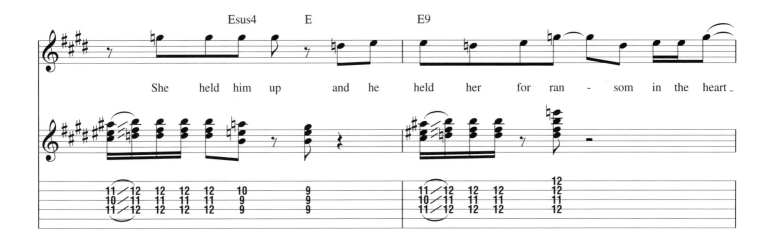

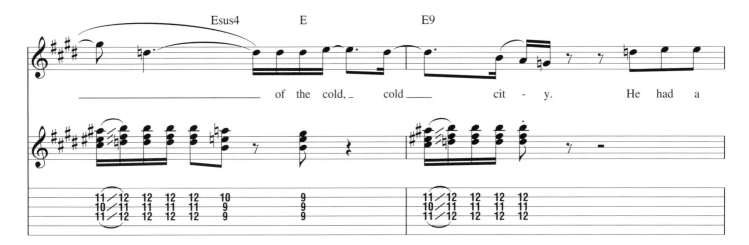

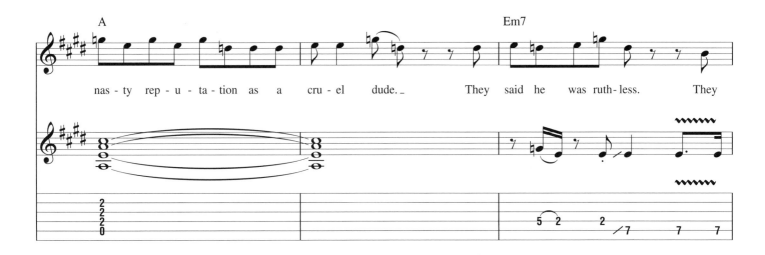

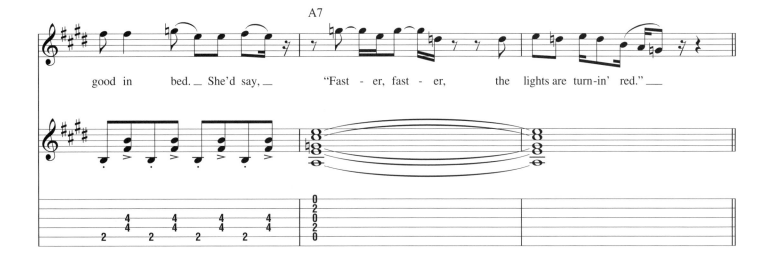

good in   bed. __ She'd say, __   "Fast - er, fast - er,   the lights are turn-in' red." __

Chorus

(Life   in the fast __ lane.

Sure - ly make __ you lose __ your   mind. __

Life   in the fast __ lane.)

Yeah. __

Interlude

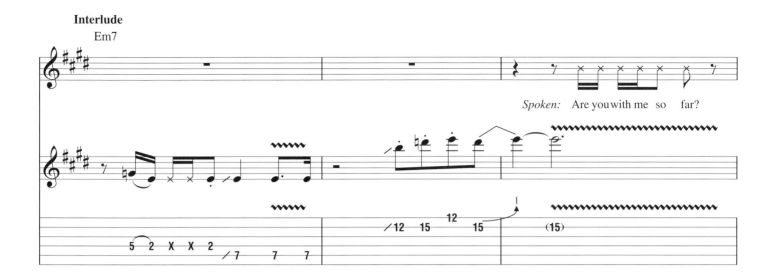

Spoken: Are you with me so far?

Verse

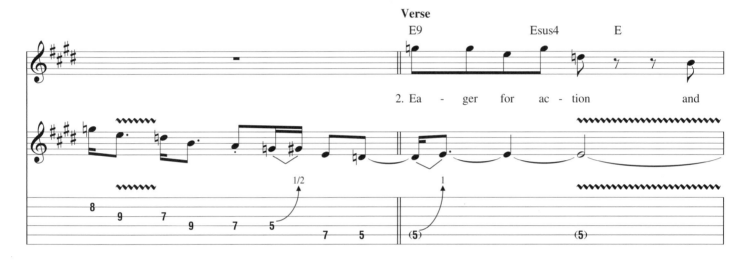

2. Ea - ger for ac - tion and

hot for the game.___ The com - ing at - trac - tion, the drop of a name.___ They knew

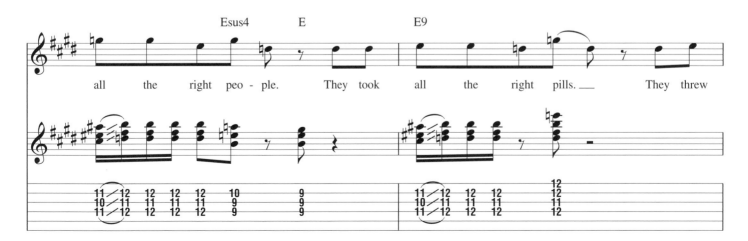

all the right peo - ple. They took all the right pills.___ They threw

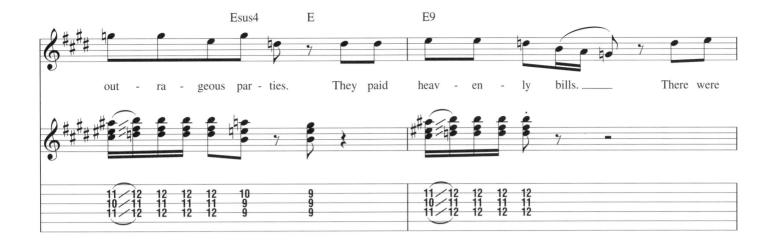

out - ra - geous par - ties. They paid heav - en - ly bills. ___ There were

lines ___ on the mir - ror, lines ___ on her face. ___ She pre -

tend - ed not to no - tice, ___ she was caught up in the race. ___

Out ev - 'ry eve - ning un - til it was light. ___ He was

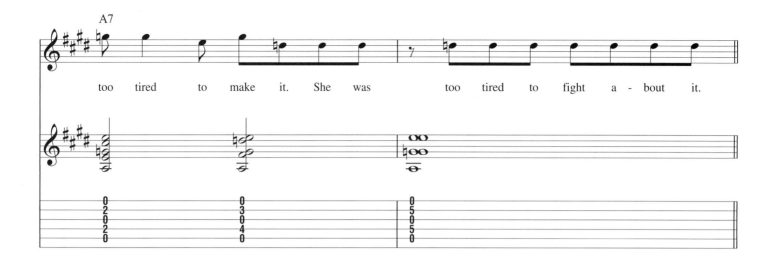

too tired to make it. She was too tired to fight a - bout it.

℅ Chorus

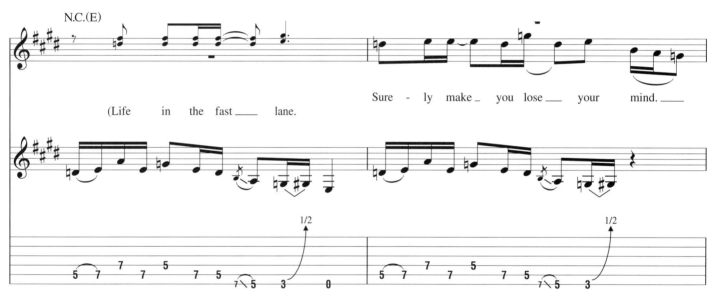

(Life in the fast ___ lane.

Sure - ly make ___ you lose ___ your mind. ___

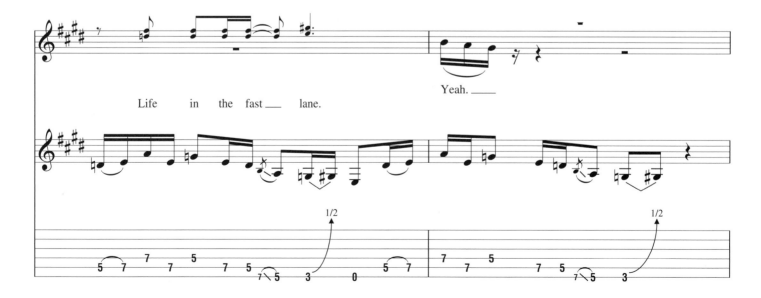

Life in the fast ___ lane.

Yeah. ___

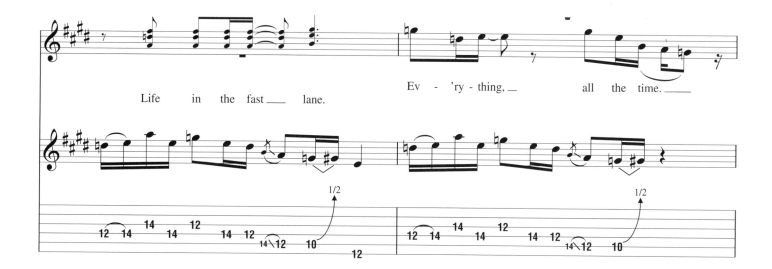

Life in the fast ___ lane.

Ev - 'ry - thing, ___ all the time. ___

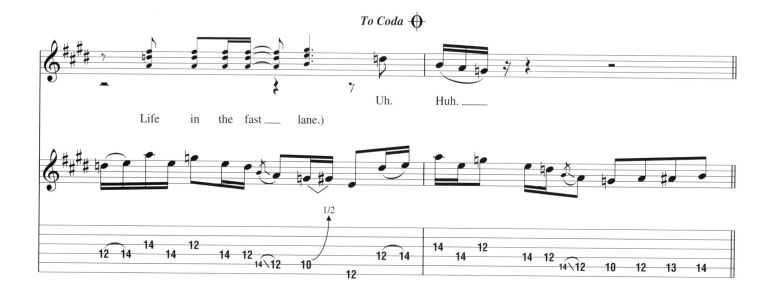

To Coda ⊕

Life in the fast ___ lane.)

Uh. Huh. ___

Guitar Solo

grad. bend

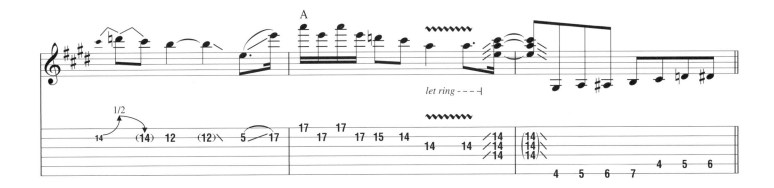

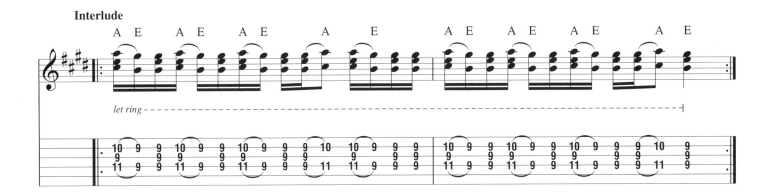

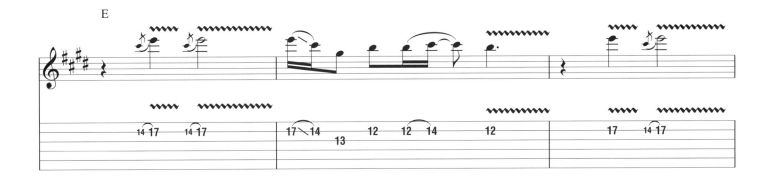

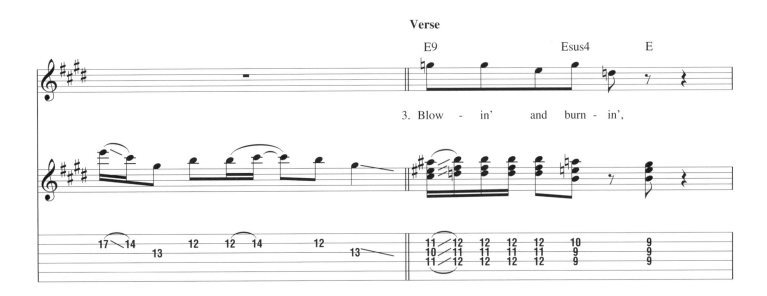

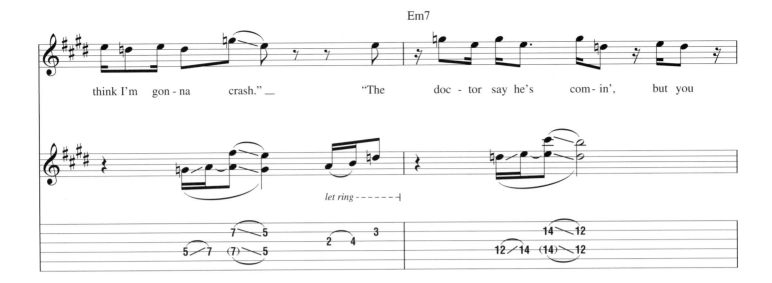

think I'm gon-na crash." __ "The doc-tor say he's com-in', but you

got-ta pay him in cash." ___ They went rush-in' down __ that free - way. Messed a-

D.S. al Coda

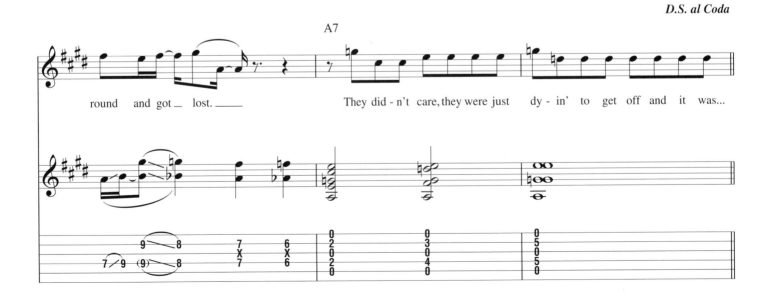

round and got __ lost. ___ They did-n't care, they were just dy - in' to get off and it was...

Coda

Interlude

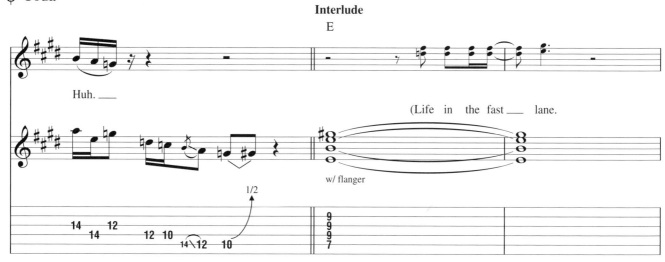

Huh. ___

(Life in the fast ___ lane.

w/ flanger

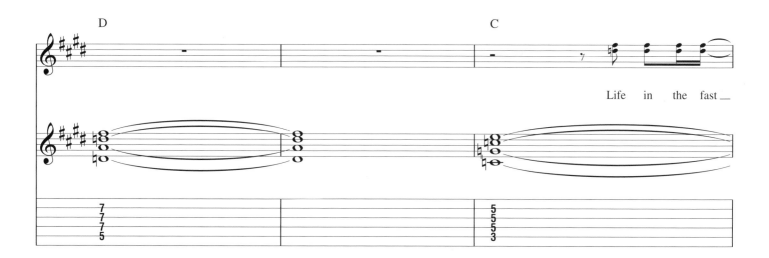

Life in the fast ___

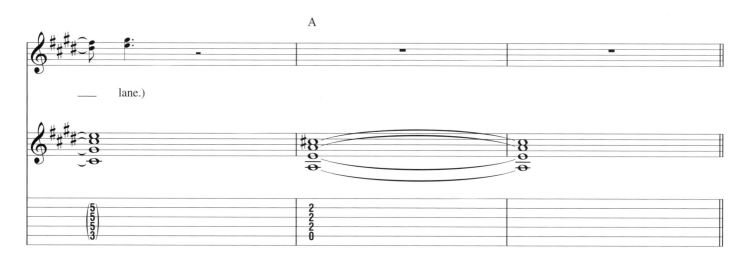

___ lane.)

Outro-Guitar Solo

N.C.(E7)

flanger off

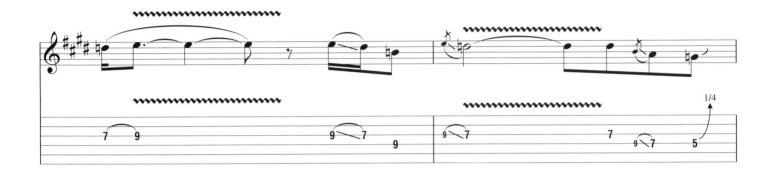

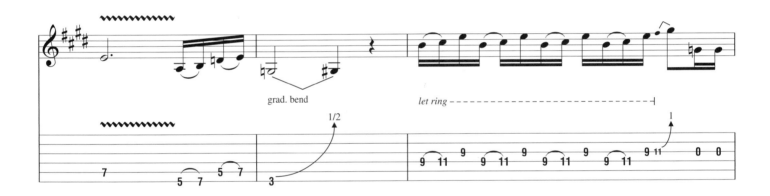

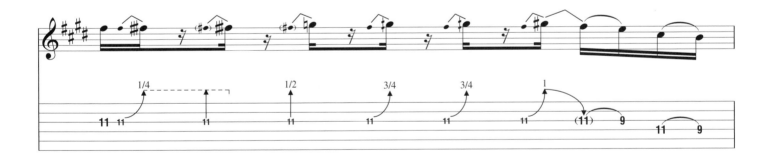

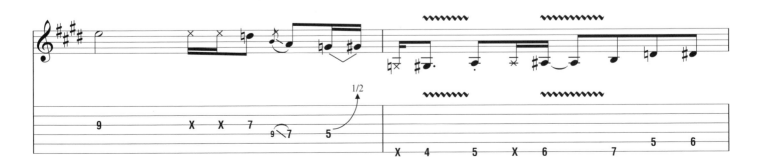

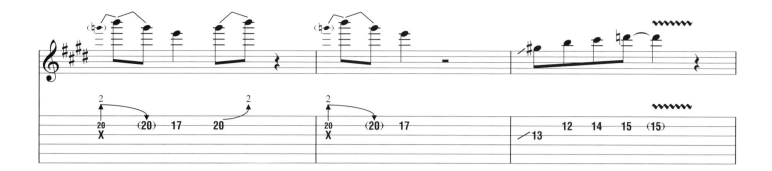

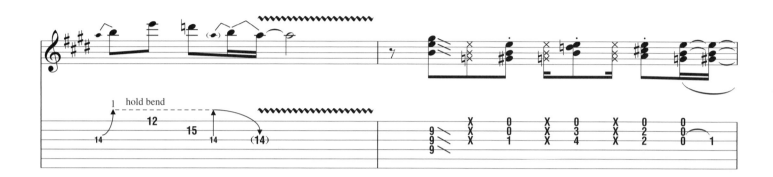

Begin fade

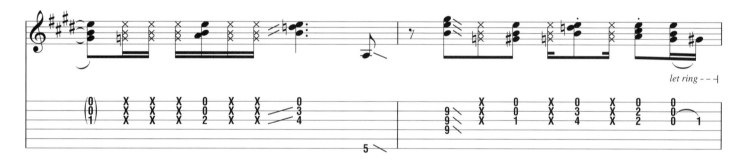

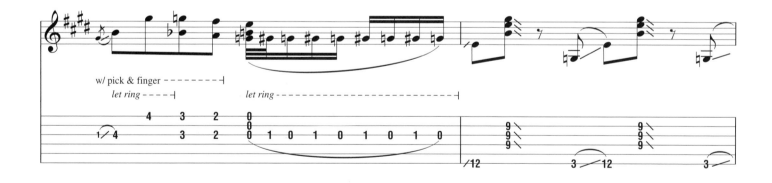

Fade out

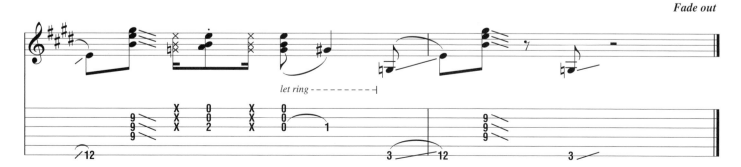

The Long Run

Words and Music by Don Henley and Glenn Frey

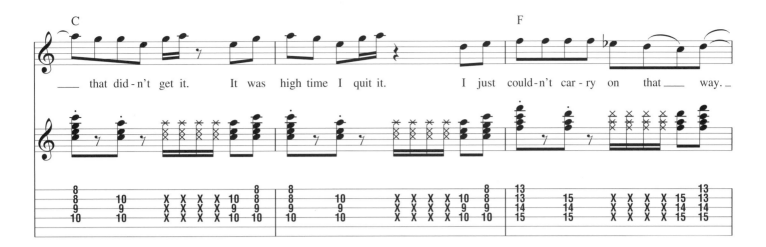

_____ that did-n't get it.   It was high time I quit it.   I just could-n't car-ry on that ___ way. _

Pre-Chorus

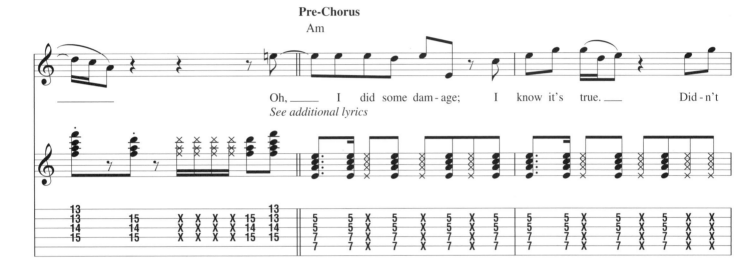

Oh, _____ I did some dam-age;   I know it's true. ___   Did-n't
See additional lyrics

Chorus

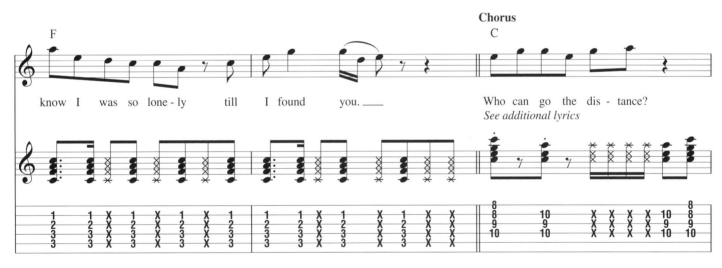

know I was so lone-ly   till I found you. ___   Who can go the dis-tance?
See additional lyrics

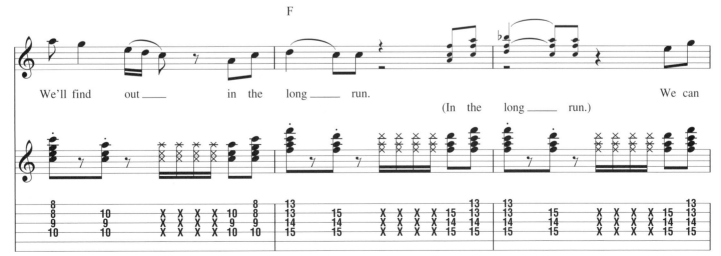

We'll find   out ___   in the long ___ run.   We can
(In the long ___ run.)

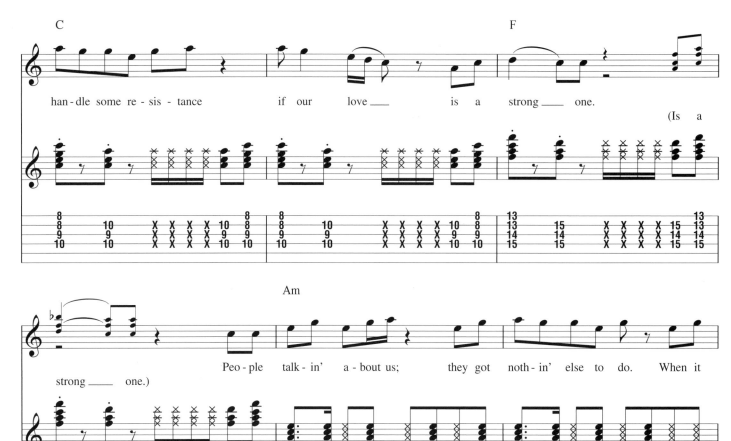

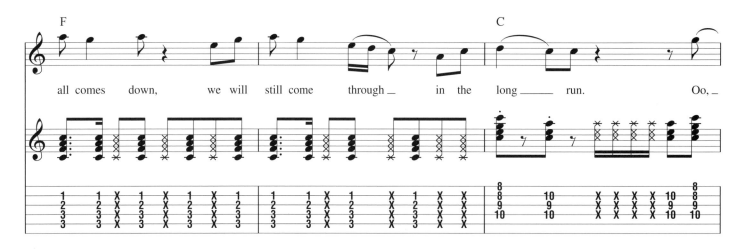

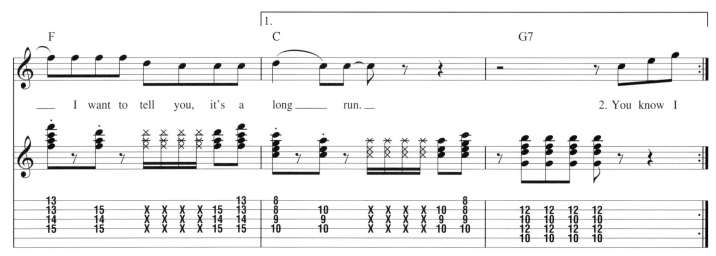

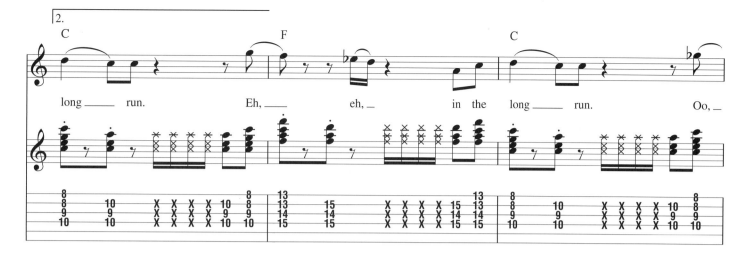

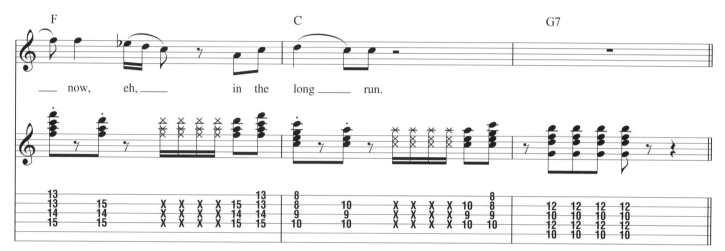

Outro-Guitar Solo

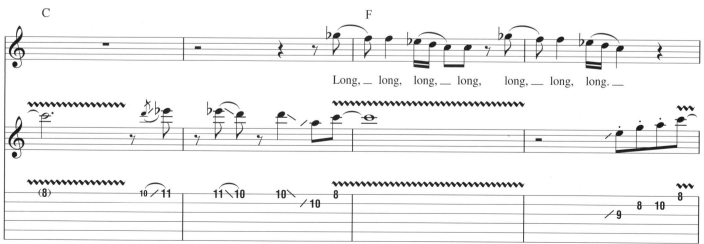

Additional Lyrics

2. You know I don't understand why you don't treat yourself better, do the crazy things that you do.
'Cause all the debutantes in Houston, baby, couldn't hold a candle to you.

Pre-Chorus Did you do it for love? Did you do it for money? Did you do it for spite? Did you think you had to, honey?

Chorus Who is gonna make it? We'll find out in the long run. (In the long run.)
I know we can take it if our love is a strong one. (Is a strong one.)
Well, we're scared, but we ain't shakin'. Kind of bent, but we ain't breakin' in the long run.
Oo, I want to tell you, it's a long run. Eh, eh, in the long run. Oo, now, eh, in the long run.

Those Shoes

Words and Music by Don Henley, Glenn Frey and Don Felder

Intro
Moderately slow ♩ = 78

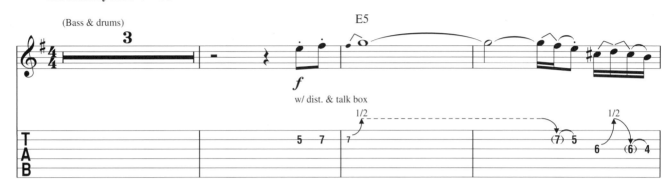

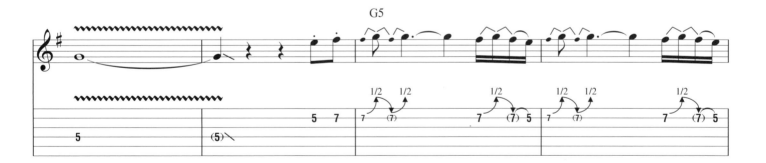

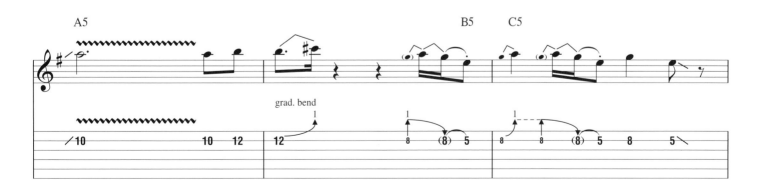

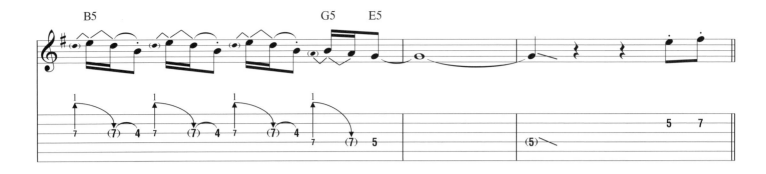

Verse

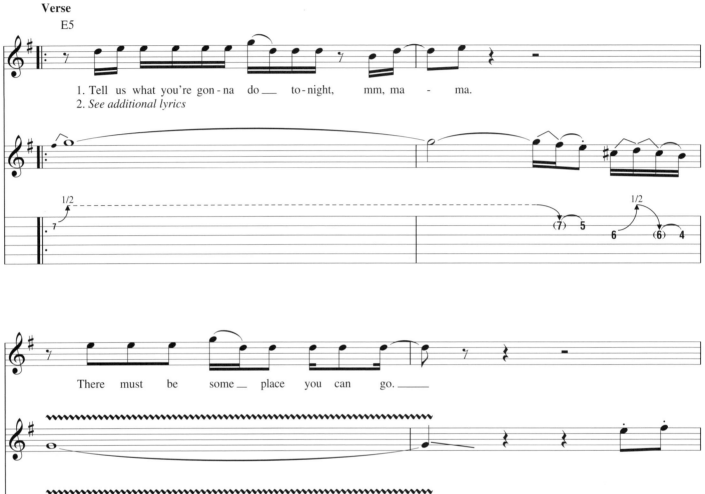

1. Tell us what you're gon - na do ___ to - night, mm, ma ___ ma.
2. *See additional lyrics*

There must be some ___ place you can go. _____

In the mid - dle of the tall ___ drinks and the dra - ma,

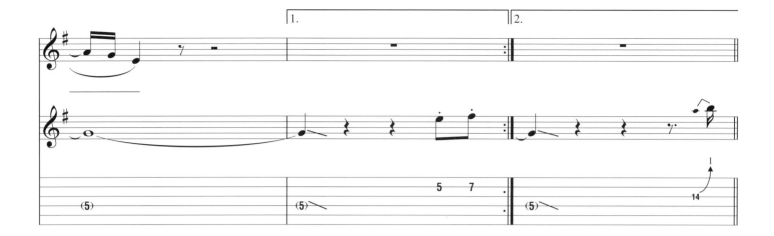

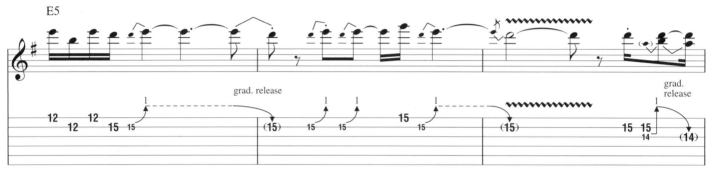

Guitar Solo

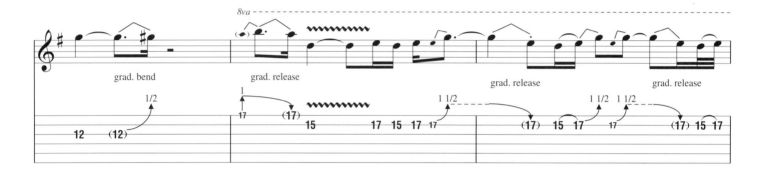

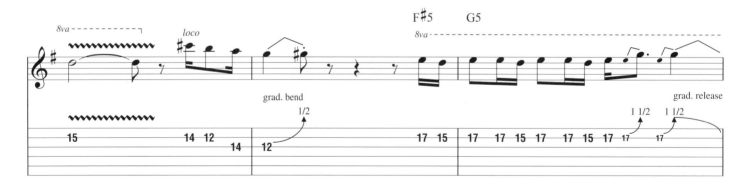

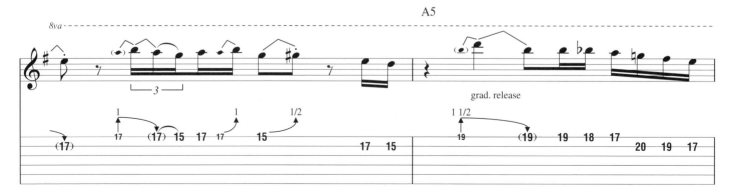

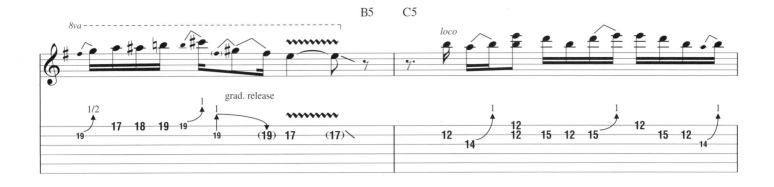

B5   C5

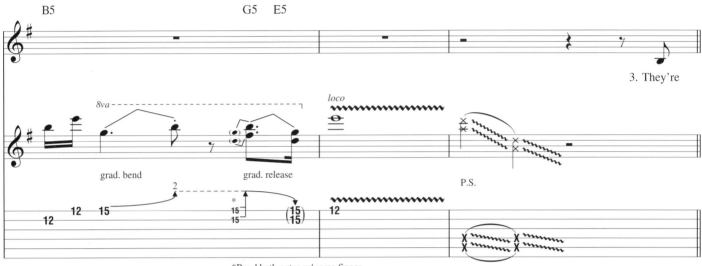

B5   G5   E5

3. They're

*Bend both notes w/ same finger.

Verse

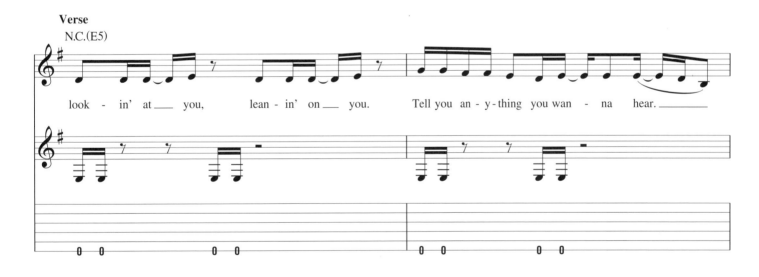

look - in' at ___ you,   lean - in' on ___ you.   Tell you an - y - thing you wan - na   hear. _____

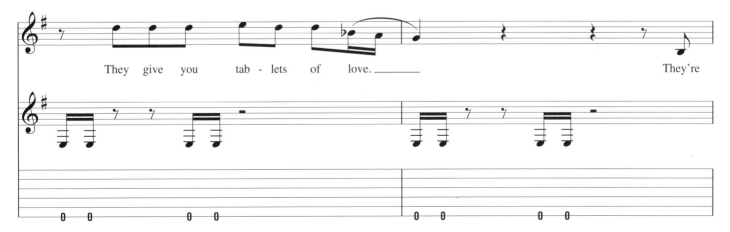

They   give   you   tab - lets   of   love. _____   They're

Additional Lyrics

2. Got those pretty little straps around your ankles, got those shiny little chains around your heart.
   You got to have your independence, hmm, but you don't know just where to start.
   Desperation in the singles bars, and all the jerkoffs in their fancy cars, you can't believe your reviews.
   Oh no, you can't do that once you've started wearin' those shoes.

One of These Nights

Words and Music by Don Henley and Glenn Frey

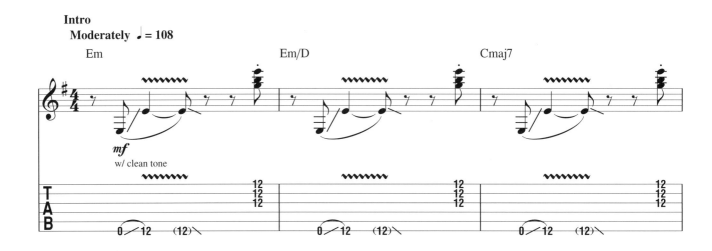

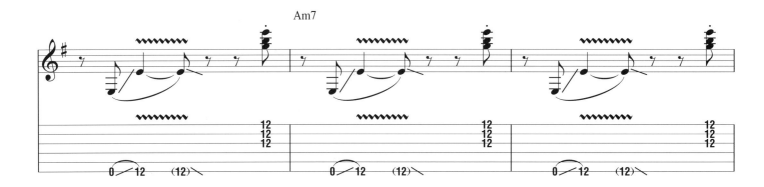

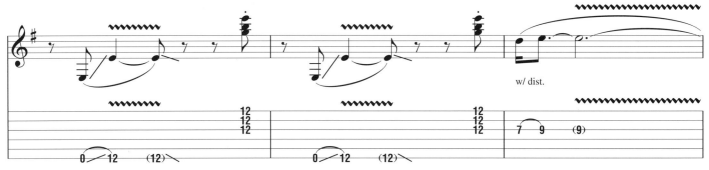

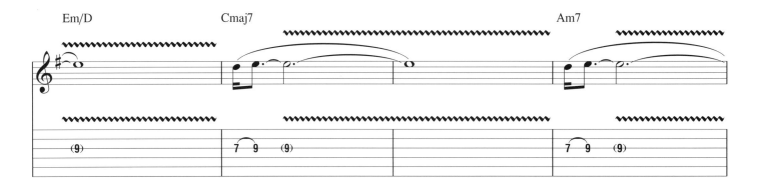

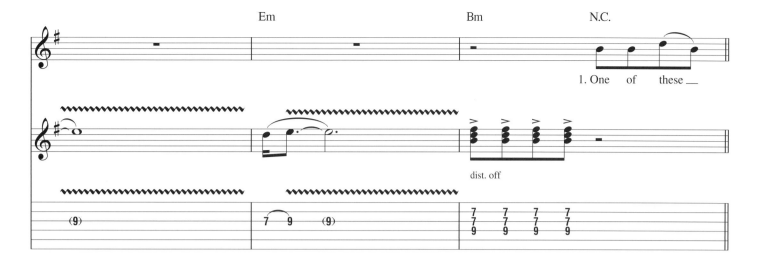

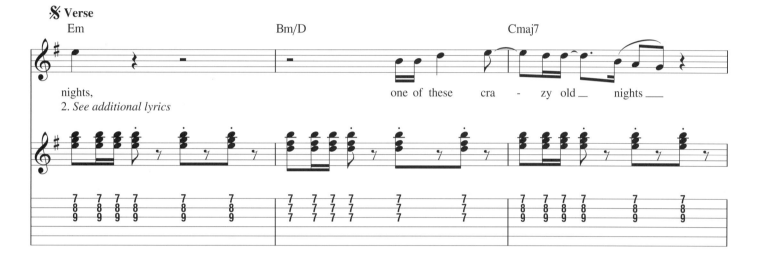

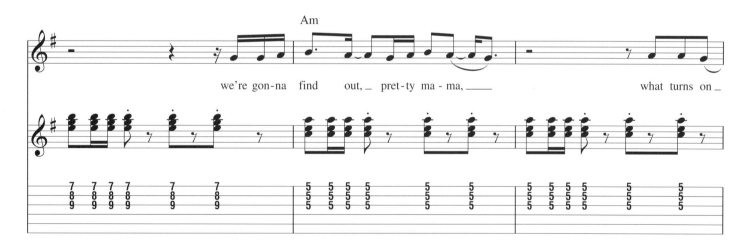

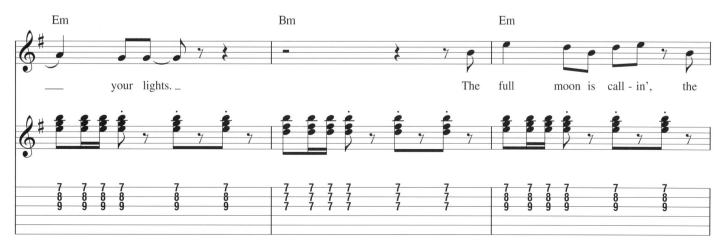

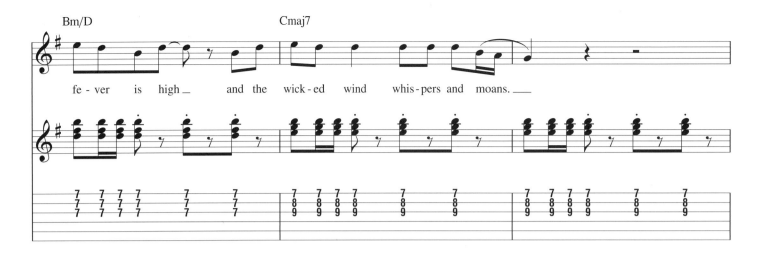

fe - ver is high ___ and the wick - ed wind whis - pers and moans. ___

You got your de - mons, and you got de - sires; ___ well, I ___ got a few of my own. ___

To Coda

Chorus

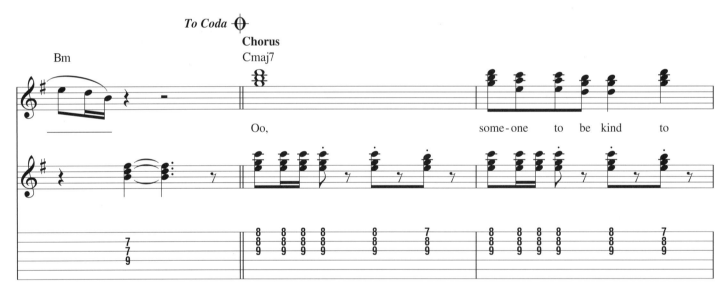

___ Oo, some - one to be kind to

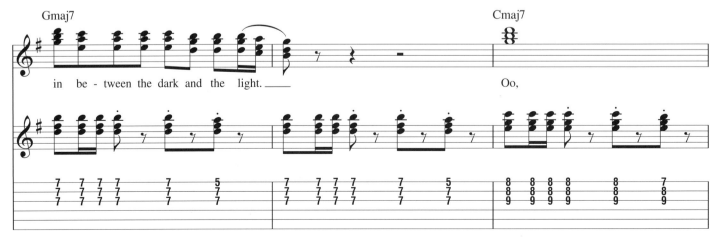

in be - tween the dark and the light. ___ Oo,

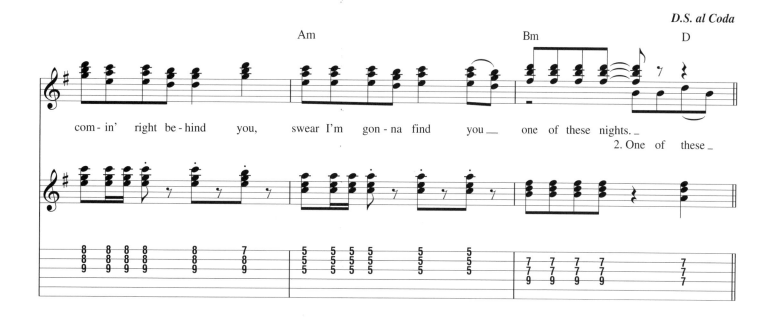

com - in' right be - hind you, swear I'm gon - na find you __ one of these nights. _

2. One of these _

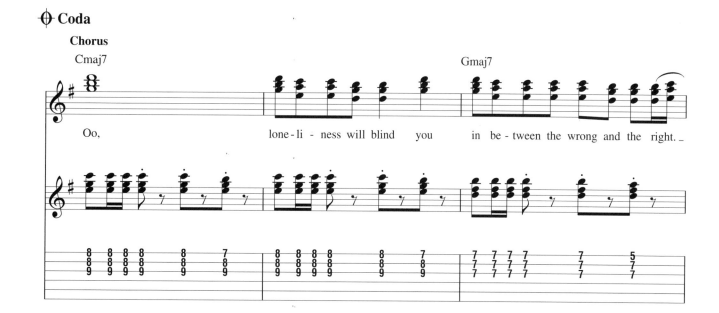

Coda

Chorus

Oo, lone - li - ness will blind you in be - tween the wrong and the right. _

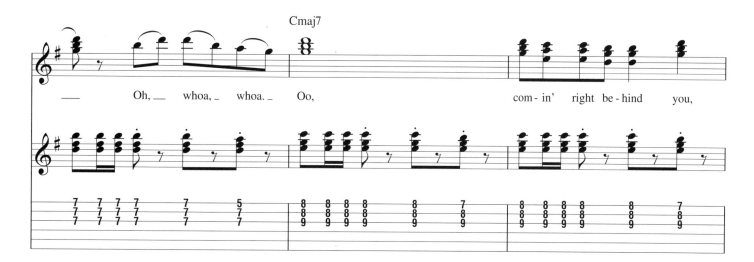

Oh, __ whoa, _ whoa. _ Oo, com - in' right be - hind you,

swear I'm gon - na find you ___ one of these nights. _

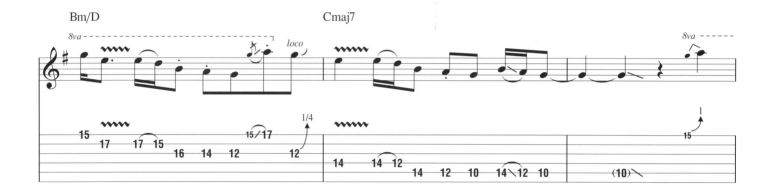

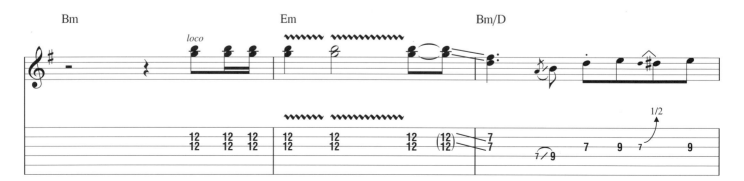

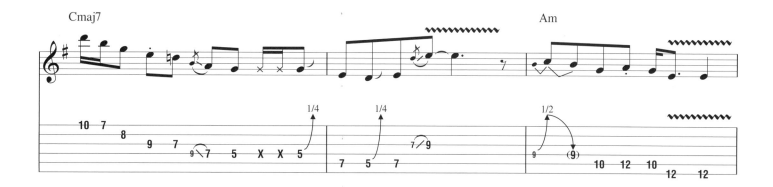

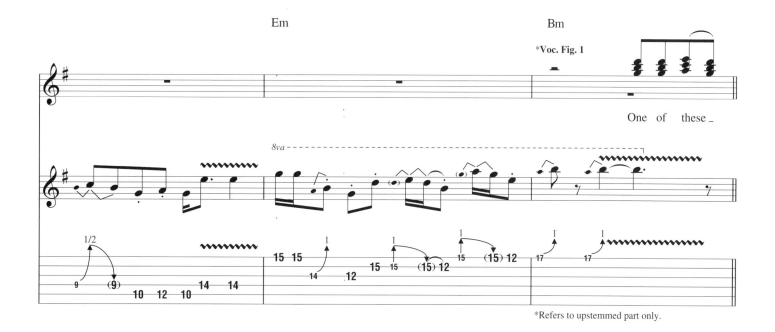

*Refers to upstemmed part only.

Outro-Chorus

Com-in' right be-hind you, swear I'm gon-na find you. ___

w/ Voc. Fig. 1

Gmaj7   Cmaj7

Get you,   ba - by, one of these nights. ___

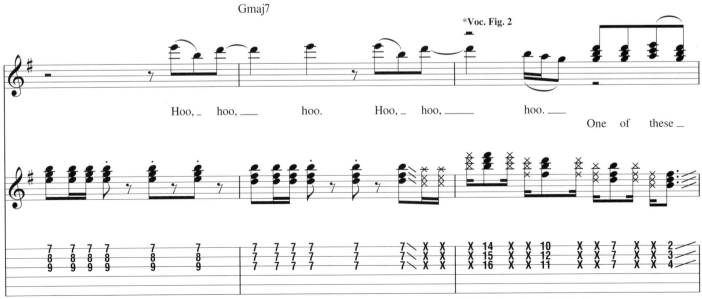

Gmaj7

*Voc. Fig. 2

Hoo, _ hoo, ___ hoo.   Hoo, _ hoo, ____ hoo. ___   One of these __

*Refers to upstemmed part only.

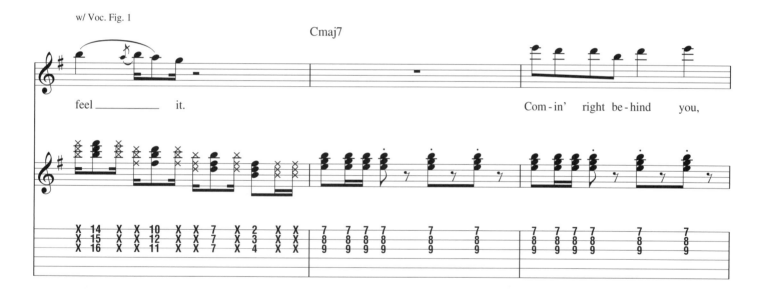

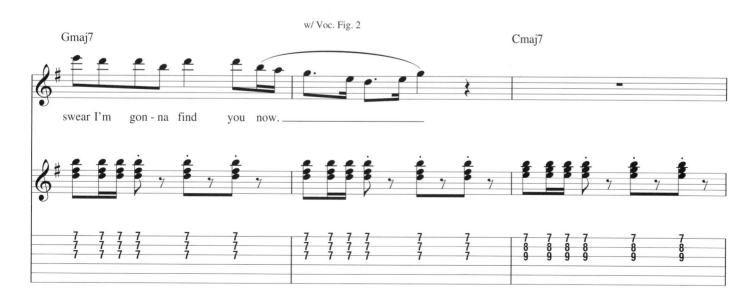

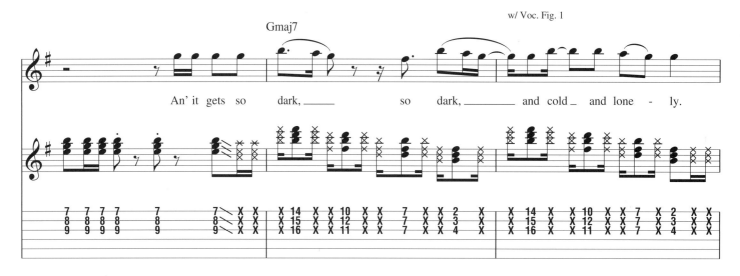

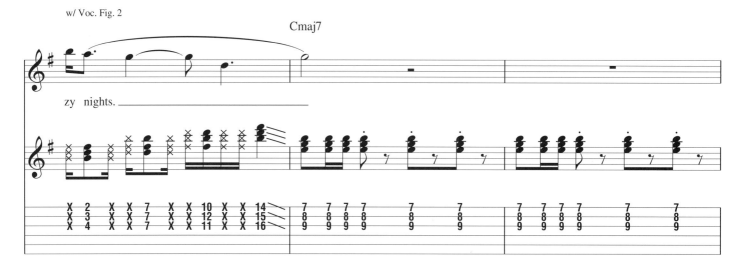

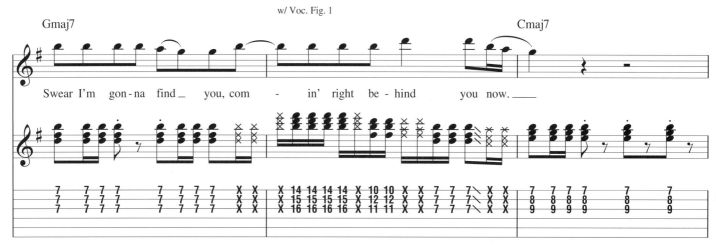

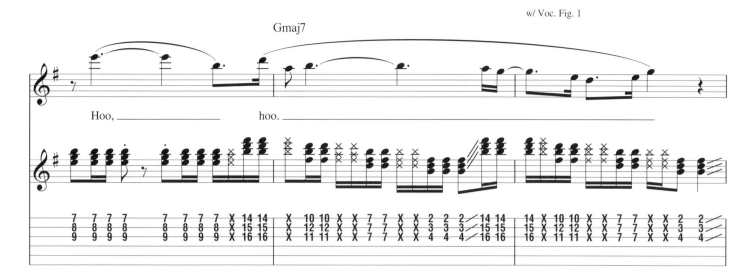

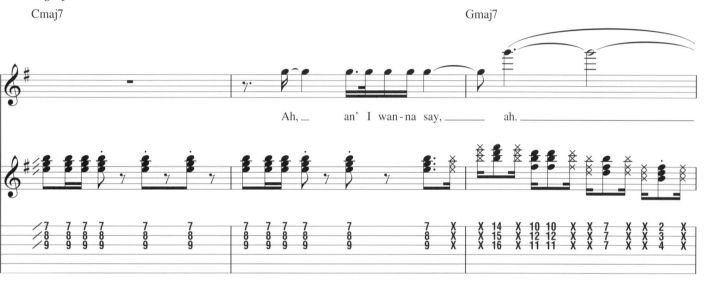

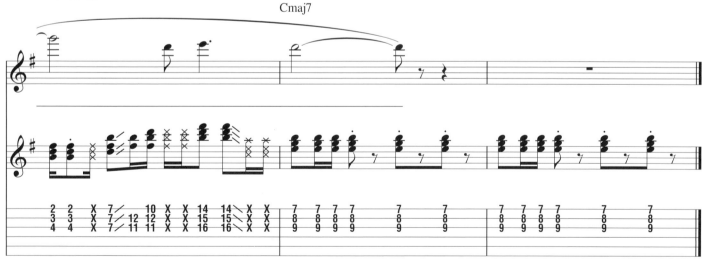

Additional Lyrics

2. One of these dreams,
   One of these lost and lonely dreams, now,
   We're gonna find one, mm, one that really screams.
   I've been searchin' for the daughter of the devil himself,
   I've been searchin' for an angel in white.
   I've been waitin' for a woman who's a little of both,
   And I can feel her but she's nowhere in sight.

Witchy Woman

Words and Music by Don Henley and Bernie Leadon

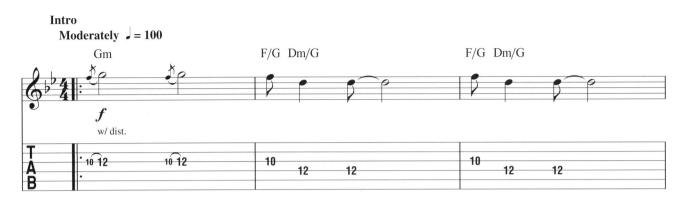

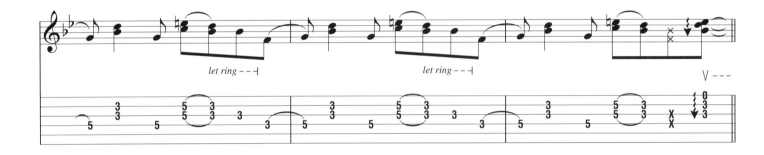

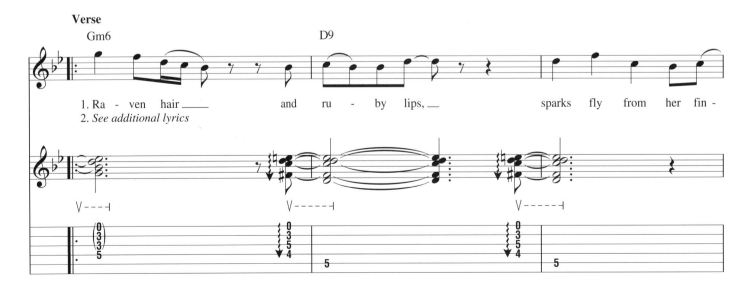

1. Ra - ven hair ___ and ru - by lips, ___ sparks fly from her fin-
2. *See additional lyrics*

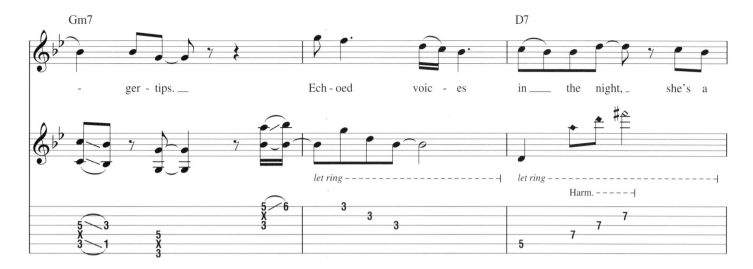

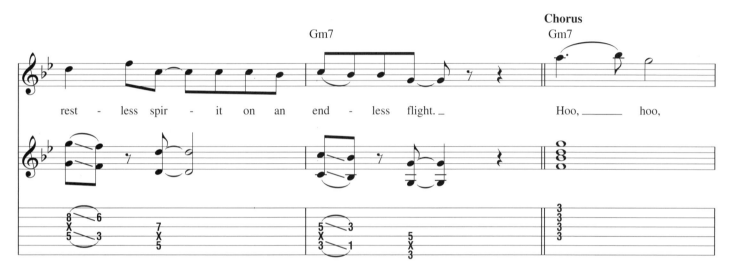

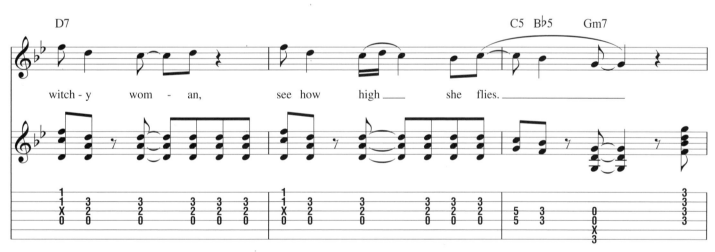

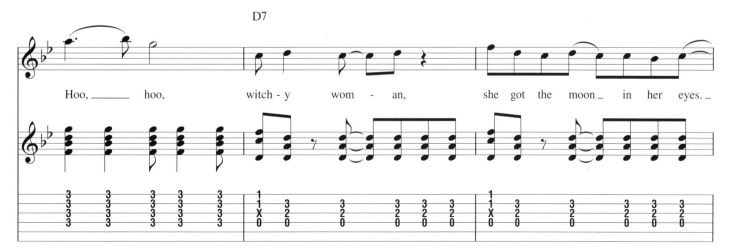

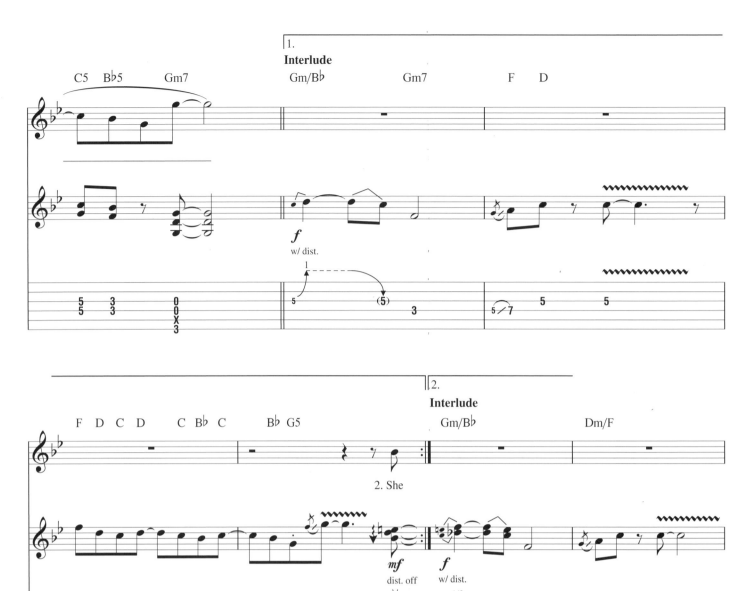

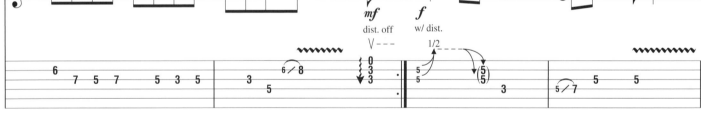

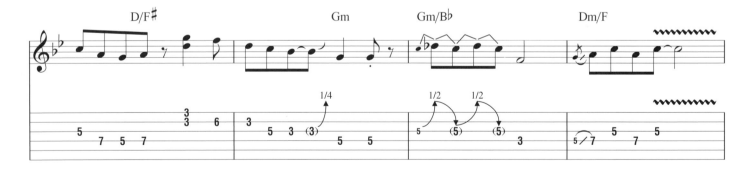

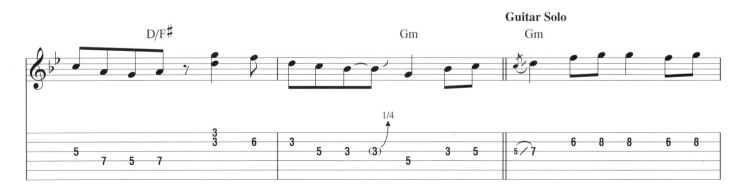

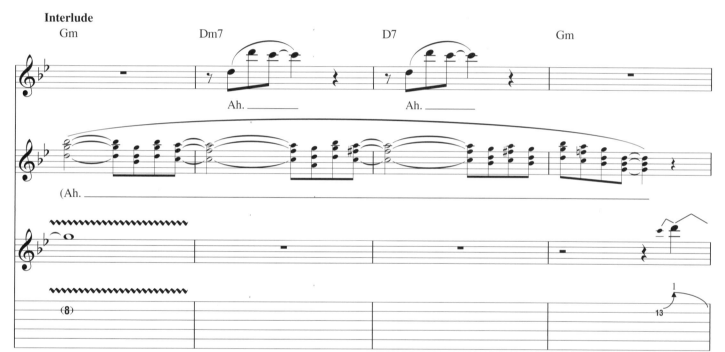

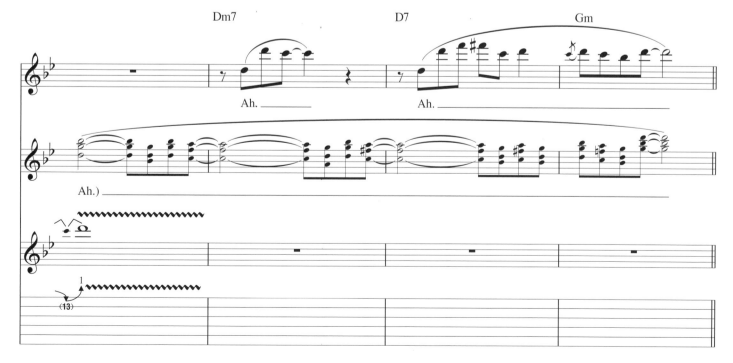

Additional Lyrics

2. She held me spellbound in the night,
Dancing shadows an' firelight.
Crazy laughter in another room,
An' she drove herself to madness with a silver spoon.

GUITAR NOTATION LEGEND

THE MUSICAL STAFF shows pitches and rhythms and is divided by bar lines into measures. Pitches are named after the first seven letters of the alphabet.

TABLATURE graphically represents the guitar fingerboard. Each horizontal line represents a string, and each number represents a fret.

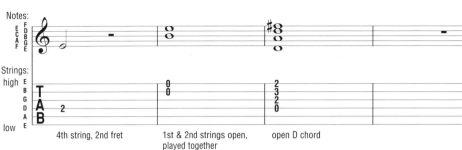

4th string, 2nd fret | 1st & 2nd strings open, played together | open D chord

HALF-STEP BEND: Strike the note and bend up 1/2 step.

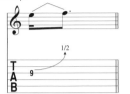

WHOLE-STEP BEND: Strike the note and bend up one step.

GRACE NOTE BEND: Strike the note and immediately bend up as indicated.

SLIGHT (MICROTONE) BEND: Strike the note and bend up 1/4 step.

BEND AND RELEASE: Strike the note and bend up as indicated, then release back to the original note. Only the first note is struck.

PRE-BEND: Bend the note as indicated, then strike it.

VIBRATO: The string is vibrated by rapidly bending and releasing the note with the fretting hand.

PALM MUTING: The note is partially muted by the pick hand lightly touching the string(s) just before the bridge.

HAMMER-ON: Strike the first (lower) note with one finger, then sound the higher note (on the same string) with another finger by fretting it without picking.

PULL-OFF: Place both fingers on the notes to be sounded. Strike the first note and without picking, pull the finger off to sound the second (lower) note.

LEGATO SLIDE: Strike the first note and then slide the same fret-hand finger up or down to the second note. The second note is not struck.

SHIFT SLIDE: Same as legato slide, except the second note is struck.

TRILL: Very rapidly alternate between the notes indicated by continuously hammering on and pulling off.

TAPPING: Hammer ("tap") the fret indicated with the pick-hand index or middle finger and pull off to the note fretted by the fret hand.

NATURAL HARMONIC: Strike the note while the fret-hand lightly touches the string directly over the fret indicated.

PINCH HARMONIC: The note is fretted normally and a harmonic is produced by adding the edge of the thumb or the tip of the index finger of the pick hand to the normal pick attack.

TREMOLO PICKING: The note is picked as rapidly and continuously as possible.

VIBRATO BAR DIVE AND RETURN: The pitch of the note or chord is dropped a specified number of steps (in rhythm), then returned to the original pitch.

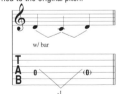

VIBRATO BAR SCOOP: Depress the bar just before striking the note, then quickly release the bar.

VIBRATO BAR DIP: Strike the note and then immediately drop a specified number of steps, then release back to the original pitch.

Additional Musical Definitions

(accent) • Accentuate note (play it louder).

(staccato) • Play the note short.

D.S. al Coda • Go back to the sign (𝄋), then play until the measure marked "***To Coda***," then skip to the section labelled "**Coda**."

D.C. al Fine • Go back to the beginning of the song and play until the measure marked "***Fine***" (end).

Fill

N.C.

• Label used to identify a brief melodic figure which is to be inserted into the arrangement.

• Harmony is implied.

• Repeat measures between signs.

• When a repeated section has different endings, play the first ending only the first time and the second ending only the second time.